Sustainability Standards and Instruments

Sustainability Standards and Instruments

Alan S. Gutterman

BEP

BUSINESS EXPERT PRESS

Leader in applied, concise business books

Sustainability Standards and Instruments

Cover design by Charlene Kronstedt

Interior design by Exeter Premedia Services Private Ltd., Chennai, India

First published in 2021 by
Business Expert Press, LLC
222 East 46th Street, New York, NY 10017
www.businessexpertpress.com

ISBN-13: 978-1-95334-988-0 (paperback)
ISBN-13: 978-1-95334-989-7 (e-book)

Business Expert Press Environmental and Social Sustainability
for Business Advantage Collection

Collection ISSN: 2327-333X (print)
Collection ISSN: 2327-3348 (electronic)

First edition: 2021

10 9 8 7 6 5 4 3 2 1

Description

It is becoming increasingly clear that firms can contribute to their own wealth and to overall societal wealth by considering the effect they have on the world at large when making decisions and take operational actions to execute their strategies. All of this has led to growing interest in "corporate social responsibility," or "CSR," which has been described as the way that firms integrate social, environmental, and economic concerns into their values, culture, decision making, strategy, and operations in a transparent and accountable manner and thereby establish better practices within the firm, create wealth, and improve society.

The commitments and activities associated with any CSR initiative should begin with compliance with laws and regulations promulgated by the governmental entities have jurisdiction over the firm's activities; however, CSR extends well "beyond the law" to include important subjects as to which the law has not been able to keep. As a result, voluntary corporate responsibility standards developed from a variety of sources have emerged to fill the gap.

This book serves as an introduction to sustainability standards and instruments and includes chapters on initiatives of governmental and intergovernmental bodies, sectoral CSR commitments, CSR-related reporting and management standards, and securities exchanges and regulators.

Keywords

sustainability; sustainability standards; CSR

Contents

CHAPTER 1

Introduction

Academics, policy makers, businesspeople, members of civil society, and individuals have all recognized the significant effect the activities of the private sector have on employees, customers, communities, the environment, competitors, business partners, investors, shareholders, governments, and others. It is also becoming increasingly clear that firms can contribute to their own wealth and to overall societal wealth by considering the effect they have on the world at large when making decisions and take operational actions to execute their strategies. All of this has led to growing interest in "corporate social responsibility" (CSR), which has been described as the way that firms integrate social, environmental, and economic concerns into their values, culture, decision making, strategy, and operations in a transparent and accountable manner and thereby establish better practices within the firm, create wealth, and improve society.[1]

The commitments and activities associated with any CSR initiative should begin with compliance with laws and regulations promulgated by the governmental entities have jurisdiction over the firm's activities; however, CSR extends well "beyond the law" to include corporate governance and ethics; health and safety; environmental stewardship; human rights (including core labor rights); sustainable development; working conditions (including safety and health, hours of work, wages); industrial relations; community involvement, development, and investment; involvement of and respect for diverse cultures and disadvantaged peoples; corporate philanthropy and employee volunteering; consumer issues, customer satisfaction, and adherence to principles of fair competition;

---

[1] For further discussion, see Gutterman, A. 2019. *Responsible Business: A Guide to Corporate Social Responsibility for Sustainable Entrepreneurs.* Oakland CA: Sustainable Entrepreneurship Project.

anti-bribery and anti-corruption measures; accountability, transparency, and performance reporting; and supplier relations, for both domestic and international supply chains. The law has not been able to keep up and the gap has been filled by CSR standards promulgated from a variety of sources.

According to Williams, most of the corporate responsibility standards are voluntary, although India passed legislation in 2014 that required companies to establish a corporate responsibility committee at the board level and contribute 2 percent of net profits to corporate responsibility initiatives.[2] It should not be forgotten, however, that many of the topics generally included within the general subject of CSR have previously been addressed to some degree in domestic regulations covering labor rights, environmental and consumer protection, anti-discrimination, and anti-bribery. Countries vary in the degree to which regulatory standards relating to corporate responsibility are relied upon and Williams noted that empirical evidence suggested that the underlying regulatory standards effectively shape the sustainability culture within countries, and have both a strong effect on how companies handle corporate responsibility issues and a strong effect on the sustainability. For example, Williams pointed out that Matten and Moon have argued that

> in countries with stakeholder corporate governance systems and more expansive social welfare arrangements, corporate responsibility is 'implicit' in doing business according to law, so companies do not need to be as 'explicit' about taking on social responsibilities, as do leading companies in more shareholder-oriented countries.[3]

Since the late 1990s there has been a proliferation of transnational, voluntary standards for what constitutes responsible corporate action

---

[2] Williams, C. 2016. "Corporate Social Responsibility and Corporate Governance." In *Oxford Handbook of Corporate Law and Governance*, eds. J. Gordon and G. Ringe, 13. Oxford: Oxford University Press, Available at http://digitalcommons.osgoode.yorku.ca/scholarly_works/1784

[3] Id. (citing Matten, D., and J. Moon. 2008. "'Implicit' and 'Explicit' CSR: A Conceptual Framework for a Comparative Understanding of Corporate Social Responsibility." *Academy of Management Review* 33, no. 2, 404).

including standards have been developed by states; public–private partnerships; multistakeholder negotiation processes; industries and companies; institutional investors; functional groups such as accountancy firms and social assurance consulting groups; nongovernmental organizations (NGOs); and nonfinancial ratings agencies.[4] Influential multilateral initiatives have included the Organisation for Economic Co-operation and Development's (OECD) Guidelines for Multinational Enterprises, the ISO 26000 Guidance on Social Responsibility, the UN Global Compact and the "Protect, Respect and Remedy" framework in the UN's Guiding Principles on Business and Human Rights that articulates the human rights responsibilities of states and companies, and notable multisector standards initiatives have included Social Accountability 8000 and the Ethical Trading Institute.[5] The common practice of relying on major international conventions and agreements on human rights, labor, corruption, the environment, and supply chains, such as those mentioned previously, has led to convergence among many of the voluntary standards with respect to the key topics covered and language used in those instruments, and convergence has also been fueled by the widespread adoption of initiatives such as the Global Reporting Initiative guidelines and the International Finance Corporation Performance Standards.[6]

Role of the State in CSR

Giovannucci et al. observed that governments have tended to focus on traditional lawmaking activities such as basic guarantees or regulations

---

[4] Id.

[5] Id. at 8–9.

[6] Wokeck, L. 2010. *Convergence and Coherence in International CSR Instruments: Implications for Business in the Asian and Pacific Region*, 68–77, https://unescap.org/sites/default/files/8%20-%20Chapter%20IV_Convergence%20and%20coherence%20CSR%20instruments_0.pdf The appendices to the ISO 26000 Guidance on Social Responsibility include extensive lists of examples of cross-sectoral initiatives as of the date ISO 26000 was completed and tables identifying the ISO 26000 core subjects and practices for integrating social responsibility that have been incorporated into the listed initiatives. ISO 26000 Guidance on Social Responsibility (Geneva: International Organization for Standardization) 87–97.

relating contract rules and food safety as opposed to getting directly involved in encouraging the development of CSR as a complementary tool for public policy.[7] However, commentators have suggested that governments can and should play a more active and supportive role in strengthen CSR in the private sector. For example, a 2002 World Bank report identified four potential key public sector roles for engaging with CSR: mandating, facilitating, partnering, and endorsing.[8] The same report listed 10 key themes for public-sector CSR-related activities: setting and ensuring compliance with minimum standards; public policy role of business; corporate governance; responsible investment; philanthropy and community development; stakeholder engagement and representation; pro-CSR production and consumption; pro-CSR certification, "beyond compliance" standards, and management systems; pro-CSR reporting and transparency; and multilateral processes, guidelines, and conventions. The report was focused primarily on developing countries and highlighted the following five key themes for future work to strengthen the CSR-related roles of public sector agencies in developing countries[9]:

- Work to build awareness of the contemporary CSR agenda within developing country agencies, including building understanding on the overall drivers, key players, and effective pressure points, as well as country-specific impact assessments of the CSR agenda for trade and investment promotion.
- Initiatives that enable public sector bodies in developing countries to become effective players in setting the terms of the CSR debate and its associated standards.

---

[7] Giovannucci, D., O. von Hagen and J. Wozniak. 2014. "Corporate Social Responsibility and the Role of Voluntary Sustainability Standards." In *Voluntary Standards Systems*, eds. C. Schmitz-Hoffmann et al., 359–366. Berlin: Springer-Verlag.

[8] Fox, T., H. Ward and B. Howard. 2002. *Public Sector Roles in Strengthening Corporate Social Responsibility: A Baseline Study*, iii–iv. Washington DC: World Bank.

[9] Id. at iv.

- Work to build a stable and transparent environment for pro-CSR investment, including efforts to strengthen basic norms of social, environmental, and economic governance and their enforcement.
- Initiatives to engage the private sector more directly in public policy processes associated with delivery of public goods (e.g., national sustainable development or poverty reduction strategies).
- Support for public sector bodies to develop frameworks within which to assess local or national priorities in relation to CSR.

Governments also have their traditional roles with respect to important elements of CSR programs including financial and technical support for the delivery of infrastructure, health, and education, all of which remain primary responsibilities of the public sector notwithstanding increased involvement and participation by for-profit businesses in public–private partnerships.

An OECD report noted that governments had supported an expansive international normative framework that included the Universal Declaration of Human Rights, the International Labor Organization (ILO) Conventions, the ILO Tripartite Declaration of Principles Concerning Multinational Enterprises and Social Policy, and the ILO Declaration on Fundamental Principles and Rights at Work, and pointed out that these instruments have become that basis for specific and comprehensive obligations for businesses operating within the private sector with respect to human rights, working conditions, and industrial relations and sustainable development.[10] The same OECD report identified

---

[10] "Overview of Selected Initiatives and Instruments Relevant to Corporate Social Responsibility," in Annual Report on the OECD Guidelines for Multinational Enterprises 2008 (Paris: Organisation for Economic Co-operation and Development, 2009), 235, 248–249. The OECD report was written in 2009 and included several other instruments that have since lapsed in formulation of the international normative framework including the 1992 Rio Declaration, the Millennium Development Goals, the Johannesburg Declaration on Sustainable Development (2002) and the 2005 World Summit Outcome.

four channels by which governments have endorsed standards relevant to CSR: international instruments developed and formally agreed by governments (and also having formal support from business and labor organizations); international initiatives developed by intergovernmental bodies; international initiatives endorsed by governments and national initiatives developed and endorsed by governments.[11]

Instruments Developed and Formally Agreed by Governments

This category includes international conventions and declarations that reflect agreed international normative principles and are directed mainly to governments for domestic implementation. Well-known and widely recognized examples of standards in this category are the ILO Declaration on Fundamental Principles and Rights at Work, which has the support of a body with universal and tripartite members, the OECD Convention on Combating Bribery of Foreign Officials in International Business Transactions, which have been developed by the OECD members and additional non-OECD countries, the Universal Declaration of Human Rights, and the UN Millennium Development Goals. Examples of more modest guidelines, limited to a single sector and developed by a limited number of governments with input from business and civil society, include the Extractive Industries Transparency Initiative and the Voluntary Principles on Security and Human Rights. While directed at governments and generally derived from wide-recognized treaties, these initiatives can also be referenced by businesses as guides for how they should conduct their operations and what they should include in their own mission and policy statements and codes of conduct. These initiatives also benefit from participation by social partners (i.e., businesses, employer organizations, trade unions and civil society organizations) in the development and implementation process.[12]

---

[11] Id. at 240–241.

[12] Id.

Initiatives Developed by Intergovernmental Bodies

International initiatives developed by intergovernmental bodies that have either been official agreed on or recognized by governments offer authoritative guidance to businesses regarding societal expectations regarding their responsible behavior (i.e., what to do and how to do it). Prominent examples in this category include the UN Global Compact and the International Finance Corporation Environmental and Social Standards.[13]

International Initiatives Endorsed by Governments

This category includes private, and thus voluntary, CSR initiatives that have been developed with the active participation of intergovernmental organizations and/or recognized by governments, such as International Organization for Standardization standards, the guidelines developed by the Global Reporting Initiative, Responsible Care Guidelines, ICMM Sustainable Development Principles and Electronic Industry Code of Conduct. Like the initiatives in the previous category, these standards can provide guidance to businesses regarding responsible behaviors; however, they are not necessarily derived from international norms.[14]

National Initiatives Developed and Endorsed by Governments

An example of an initiative in this category is the Ethical Trading Initiative, which was founded and developed with the support of the United Kingdom government. The OECD argued that these initiatives were important because national governments participated in the process of developing the initiatives, typically working with business, civil society and other stakeholders, and because they may ultimately be used as reference points for international initiatives and/or codes of conduct for businesses operating in those countries (or with suppliers operating in those companies).[15]

---

[13] Id.

[14] Id.

[15] Id.

Private CSR Initiatives

Private CSR initiatives provide a means for businesses to organize their efforts to go "beyond the law" in their operations to act in a manner that is consistent with societal expectations regarding responsibility. The process of creating, implementing, and monitoring private CSR initiatives allows and encourages dialogue and debate among various actors including businesses, business associations, public authorities, trade unions, intergovernmental organizations, and NGOs.[16] The CSR landscape has long been complex and multifaceted with hundreds of private initiatives with their own code or set of standards relating to social and environmental issues and substantial variation in objectives, origin, areas covered, and implementation mechanisms.[17] For example, an OECD report noted that

> some [private CSR] initiatives aim to raise awareness of the importance of corporate responsibility in general; others promote a particular code of conduct; still others focus on providing tools such as reporting guidelines or services, e.g., certification and labelling schemes.[18]

Initiatives may address a broad range of CSR-related issues or be drawn more narrowly to focus in depth on one or a few of the issues such as business and human rights or environmental standards.

The OECD report referred to earlier classified private CSR initiatives into corporate codes of conduct, multistakeholder initiatives, certification and labeling initiatives (including reporting), model codes, sectoral initiatives, international framework agreements, and socially responsible investment initiatives. While the sheer volume of initiatives can make the process of review challenging and daunting, the OECD argued that the number and diversity of initiatives available offers businesses the possibility of flexibility, avoids a "one-size fits all approach" and increases the chances that firms will be able to find support to address

---

[16] Id. at 237.

[17] Id.

[18] Id. at 237–238.

concerns of particular interest.[19] Businesses may create their own CSR guidelines (i.e., corporate codes of conduct); however, many companies publicly commit to be held accountable for adhering to industry-led or multistakeholder CSR initiatives (including submission to auditing and reporting to stakeholders on compliance).

While the various CSR standards and initiatives were developed separately and intended to operate on a "stand alone" basis, businesses can, and generally do, refer or commit to several initiatives (or parts thereof) when putting together their own codes of conduct and CSR programs. For example, businesses may integrate the provisions of the ILO Declaration on Fundamental Principles and Rights at Work, the OECD Convention on Combating Bribery of Foreign Officials in International Business Transactions and the UN Global Compact to cover a comprehensive range of labor issues including freedom of association and collective bargaining, elimination of all forms of forced or compulsory labor, abolition of child labor, nondiscrimination in employment and occupation, general development, employment promotion, training, wages and benefits, hours of work, safety and health, social protection, and industrial relations. The three initiatives can also be used for CSR-related issues other than labor including reporting and disclosure, human rights, environment, bribery, consumer interests, competition, and taxation.[20]

Giovannucci et al. noted that while voluntary standards are often lumped together into a single broad category of relevant tools for sustainability and CSR, there are clearly significant differences among them.[21] As a general rule, voluntary standards deal with issues that have not been

---

[19] Id. at 238.

[20] Id. at 242–243. See also Annex 6.A6 to the OECD Report, which sets out categories of instruments and initiatives relevant to CSR by issues covered and illustrative examples of government sponsored or supported, industry sponsored, partnership sponsored, and labor- or NGO-sponsored initiatives. Categories covered in addition to those mentioned in the text included risk, quality management and assurance, supply chain codes, certification, and labeling and engagement.

[21] Giovannucci, D., O. von Hagen and J. Wozniak. 2014. "Corporate Social Responsibility and the Role of Voluntary Sustainability Standards." In *Voluntary Standards Systems*, eds. C. Schmitz-Hoffmann et al., 359–366. Berlin: Springer-Verlag.

adequately addressed by global trading structures such as environmental and social issues, quality management, ethics, and business integrity. However, the effectiveness of the voluntary standards in general, as well as in instances of specific application by firms, depends on a variety of factors including the structure of the value chain in which production takes place; the extent to which demand for a firm's products relies on its brand identity; the possibilities for collective action by consumers, workers, or other activists; and the extent to which commercial interests of lead firms align with social and environmental concerns.[22] Giovannucci et al. also pointed out that while the sponsors of voluntary standards are well-meaning and activism-oriented, they are often understaffed and underfunded and thus ill-equipped to resolve all of the complex issues of sustainability for entire supply chains.[23]

Corporate Standards and Codes of Conduct

Codes of conduct are directive statements that provide guidance and prohibit certain kinds of conduct and which may be applicable to a company's own environmental and social impacts, the impacts of its suppliers or both. When suppliers are covered by a code, there will typically be procedures for monitoring supplier compliance. Historically, codes of conduct have been most popular in the consumer goods, food, retail, and extractive industries.[24]

Giovannucci et al. noted that some companies had elected to create their own standards and propagate their own labels either independently or as part of associations and that it was not clear whether they have had an impact in terms of global trade since they were often internal standards or sometimes primarily marketing-oriented efforts (e.g., supermarkets have

---

[22] Id. at 368 (citing Mayer, F., and G. Gereffi. 2010. "Regulation and Economic Globalization: Prospects and Limits of Private Governance." *Business Politics* 12, no. 3, p. 1).

[23] Id. at 381.

[24] "Overview of Selected Initiatives and Instruments Relevant to Corporate Social Responsibility" in Annual Report on the OECD Guidelines for Multinational Enterprises 2008 (Paris: Organisation for Economic Co-operation and Development, 2009), 235, 238.

often created their own labels as a distinctive communication to their consumers).[25] They observed that most of the association or industrywide standards, such as the Roundtable for Sustainable Palm Oil and Ethical Tea Partnership, were business-to-business (B2B) standards and tended to have broader effects in terms of raising awareness and establishing minimum guidelines. However, as Giovannucci et al. pointed out, while the B2B standards provide a useful base, most of them have been primarily concerned with quality, food safety, and traceability as opposed to social and environmental requirements and have set the bar for compliance at a fairly low level.

Giovannucci et al. concluded that most, although not all, of the standards and verification programs that have been established within the corporate arena are often excluded from discussions of voluntary standards because they generally tend to differ from the salient values of those standards in several ways: they are often imposed on producers and supply chains and rarely include the serious input of producers in their design; the lack of independent oversight or third-party certification suggests that the private firms that control them can alter, dilute, or simply not fully apply the standard at their prerogative; when lacking adequate support or remuneration for sustainable production practices, they can serve as significant barriers to entry for producers; and they are rarely transparent and if they lack accountability that engages consumers, they are limited as a market mechanism that drives sustainability.[26] Most of the largest firms, such as Wal-Mart, Nestle, Unilever, Kraft Foods, and Mars, have apparently concluded that the costs of launching their own standards did not match the benefits of such an effort and that their customers did not want them to compete in this space and preferred that they align themselves with voluntary standards as a more accepted arbiter of sustainability.[27]

---

[25] Giovannucci, D., O. von Hagen, and J. Wozniak. 2014. "Corporate Social Responsibility and the Role of Voluntary Sustainability Standards." In *Voluntary Standards Systems*, eds. C. Schmitz-Hoffmann et al., 359–369. Berlin: Springer-Verlag.

[26] Id. at 370.

[27] Id.

Certification and Labeling

Certification and labeling initiatives have been described as efforts to provide purchasers, both consumers and businesses, with information that is recognized as reliable for use in their purchasing decisions. As is the case with multistakeholder initiatives, certification and labeling can either cover a broad range of issues or may be focused on a particular CSR topic such as child labor, fair trade, or forest conservation. The ability of businesses to rely on certification or labeling is conditioned on completion of compliance audits conducted by accredited independent inspectors. If businesses fail an audit, they are generally allowed to take remedial steps in order to preserve the certification or license.[28] Examples of certification and labeling initiatives include Social Accountability 8000-Social Accountability International, ISO 14000 Series of Environmental Management Standards, Greenhouse Gas Product Certification Standard, AccountAbility AA1000 Assurance Standard, Global Reporting Initiative, Forest Stewardship Council, and Marine Stewardship Council.[29]

Model Codes

Model codes of conduct are developed by MSIs, NGOs, trade unions, or other actors and are intended to establish a minimum set of standards that can be used as a reference point by businesses seeking to create their own codes of conduct. Model codes lay out the issues that should be covered in corporate codes of conduct and thus it is not surprising that model codes are often used as a benchmark for evaluating the efforts of companies. Stakeholders such as trade unions can also use model codes of conduct to negotiate with companies.[30] Examples of model codes of conduct include Ethical Trading Initiative, Fair Labor Association Workplace Code of Conduct, ISEAL Code of Good Practice for Setting Social and Environmental Standards, International Chamber of Commerce

---

[28] "Overview of Selected Initiatives and Instruments Relevant to Corporate Social Responsibility." in Annual Report on the OECD Guidelines for Multinational Enterprises 2008 (Paris: Organisation for Economic Co-operation and Development, 2009), 235–239.

[29] Id. at 246.

[30] Id.

(ICC) Business Charter for Sustainable Development, Caux Round Table Principles for Business, ICC Guidance on Supply Chain Responsibility, Greenhouse Gas Product Certification Standard, International Social and Environmental Accreditation and Labelling Alliance, and Business Leaders Initiative for Human Rights.[31]

Sectoral Initiatives

Sector- or industrywide initiatives have been described as aiming to address widespread challenges in a specific sector (within a country, regionally, or internationally) and provide a common approach in direct operations or in dealing with supply chain management.[32] Sectoral initiatives may be led by businesses or developed through a multistakeholder process and the goal is to establish uniformity across an industry by setting a single standard that all companies can follow and apply to the operations of their suppliers (many of which have relationships with multiple purchasers in the industry). Suppliers should be engaged in the development of sector initiatives to promote uniformity, thus relieving them from the conflicts and burdens of attempting to comply with multiple individual company codes of conduct (and associated monitoring processes). Examples of sector initiatives include Electronic Industry Code of Conduct, ICC International Codes of Marketing and Advertising Practice, Responsible Care (chemical industry), International Mining and Metals Council Principles for Sustainable Development Performance, International Council of Toy Industries CARE Initiative, Forest Stewardship Council Principles and Criteria, Marine Stewardship Council Environmental Standard, and Better Cotton Initiative.[33]

---

[31] Id. at 246.

[32] Id. at 239.

[33] Id. at 247. See also Annex 6.A6 to the OECD Report, which sets out categories of instruments and initiatives relevant to CSR by sectors covered and illustrative examples of government-sponsored or supported, industry-sponsored, partnership-sponsored and labor- or NGO-sponsored initiatives in the following sectors: advertising, agriculture, apparel, chemicals, energy, extractives, investment, electrical, forestry, fisheries, oil and gas, and toys.

International Framework Agreements

International Framework Agreements (IFAs) are a special type of standard typically used by multinational companies (MNCs) with operations and supply chain partners in multiple countries. These companies may negotiate with national trade unions and global union federations to reach agreement on the labor standards that will apply to the company's operations (and its expectations of its suppliers) across the globe, regardless of the letter and enforcement of local laws.[34] While IFAs are limited to the specific MNC, as opposed to all enterprises active in the sector, they can promote worker rights at the global level and provide opportunities for both sides to discuss and reach agreement on core labor values and standards relating to wages, working conditions and health and safety in the workplace. However, MNCs must carefully consider the benefits and costs associated with entering into an IFA including the impact of local laws and customs and the ability of country-level subsidiaries to work with local unions on issues that are specific to the area and which are not adequately addressed in the more general framework agreement. In addition, terms generally found in IFAs, such as "fair wages" and "appropriate work hours," will have different meanings across countries and will need to be construed in light of applicable local laws.[35]

Socially Responsible Investment

Socially responsible investment (SRI) initiatives focus on taking social responsibility into account when an actor, such as global financial institution like the International Finance Corporation (IFC) or a private investor or bank, makes decisions about whether to invest in a particular company or project. In fact, the IFC has adopted a set of performance standards to guide its investments and these standards have

---

[34] Id. at 239.

[35] *Handbook on Corporate Social Responsibility (CSR) for Employers' Organizations.* (European Union CSR for All Project, April 2014), 31–34.

been incorporated by private banks and other financial institutions into their assessment of project finance and project-related corporate loan proposals through their commitment to adhere to the Equator Principles (equator-principles.com), which is a risk management framework adopted by financial institutions for determining, assessing, and managing environmental and social risk in projects and is primarily intended to provide a minimum standard for due diligence and monitoring to support responsible risk decision making. On the equity side, the UN Principles for Responsible Investment have been used by fund managers and other investors.[36]

Multistakeholder Initiatives

As the global economy has become more complex and trade connections have emerged that span the globe, governments have struggled to cooperate on developing new universally accepted guidelines with respect to requiring businesses to respect human rights, preserve the environment, and follow good governance practices throughout their global operations. This failure of governments has been referred to as a "governance gap" and has led companies, NGOs, and other actors to turn their attention to developing their own voluntary compliance standards that businesses can organize around including principles, management standards, and reporting indicators that are based on universal goals and aspirations memorialized in international conventions relating to human rights, labor, and the environment. The process of these collaborations has been fittingly called multistakeholder initiatives (MSIs), sometimes referred to as international multistakeholder processes, and the outputs have become important and established global governance instruments that have been

---

[36] "Overview of Selected Initiatives and Instruments Relevant to Corporate Social Responsibility." In Annual Report on the OECD Guidelines for Multinational Enterprises 2008. Paris: Organisation for Economic Co-operation and Development, 235–239.

incorporated into corporate compliance codes, government policies, and civil society initiatives.[37]

MSIs have become a popular strategy for discussing and resolving questions and conflict relating to issues of social and environmental responsibility. Multistakeholder processes have been described as decision-making bodies, voluntary or statutory, comprising two or more interest groups (i.e., stakeholders) who perceive a common problem and realize their interdependence in solving it and come together to share their views and agree on strategies and activities for collectively solving the problem.[38] The sponsors of the Multi-Stakeholder Initiative Database explained that MSIs convene actors such as corporations, civil society organizations, governments, and local communities to address challenging issues linked to the conduct of companies and governments around the world including forced labor, deforestation, and government corruption and noted that MSIs operated in almost every major global industry: certifying the production of clothing and other manufactured goods, monitoring commercial fishing practices, establishing codes of conduct for agricultural producers, and more.[39]

In their brief history of the growth and pervasiveness of voluntary standards, Giovannucci et al. reported that the first standard certification (Organic Demeter) by an independent third party was granted in 1967 to a coffee farm in a remote area of Chiapas, Mexico. Organic was later joined by Fair Trade, which emerged in the 1980s and also began with coffee. By the early years of the 2010s, Organic and Fair Trade has become

---

[37] The New Regulators? Assessing the Landscape of Multi-Stakeholder Initiatives: Findings from a database of transnational standard-setting multi-stakeholder initiatives (MSI Integrity and the Duke Human Rights Center at the Kenan Institute for Ethics, June 2017), 2.

[38] Hohnen, P., and J. Potts, ed. 2007. *Corporate Social Responsibility: An Implementation Guide for Business*. Winnipeg: International Institute for Sustainable Development. 49–50.

[39] https://msi-database.org/report. For further information on the methodology used to conduct the project, including the classification of industries and sectors, see Methodology and Classification Guide available at https://msi-database.org/methodology.

globally recognized multibillion dollar segments that had grown to covered nearly every type of agricultural product from cocoa to cheese to
cotton. The 1990s and early 2000s also saw the emergence of several other
new voluntary standards for food and agriculture, such as the Rainforest
Alliance, which Giovannucci et al. felt provided arguably less challenging
requirements in some areas and more business-friendly approaches. These
new standards were well received among large mainstream firms and they
grew much faster than Organic or Fair Trade even though they did not
have Organic's range of product coverage or its depth of market awareness
and global recognition.[40]

As voluntary standards emerged and expanded, their popularity and
acceptance among major global consumer brands also increased. By
the early 2010s, Kraft Foods, Unilever, Mars, Hershey, Chiquita, and
Cadbury had all made significant commitments to certified sourcing for
a number of their most popular brands. Further motivation for certification based on well-known voluntary standards was provided by demands
from large retailers, such as Wal-Mart and McDonalds, for organic ver-
sions of their most popular products. Giovannucci et al. reported that
coffee was the birthplace for voluntary standards and had remained the
leading commodity to apply different standards, not surprising given that
it is the world most valuable export crop. Substantial growth in voluntary
standards has also occurred for products such as bananas, tea, seafood,
and cotton.[41]

Most of the MSIs were first launched in the late 1990s and early
2000s, thus establishing a critical mass of initiatives that shared the
same basic design (e.g., formalized decision-making processes, an
agreed-upon set of standards that are meant to be mandatory for all
members and external auditing processes designed to provide some
assurance as to whether members have been complying with the

---

[40] Giovannucci, D., O. von Hagen, and J. Wozniak. 2014. "Corporate
Social Responsibility and the Role of Voluntary Sustainability Standards." In
Voluntary Standards Systems. eds. C. Schmitz-Hoffmann et al., 359–371. Berlin:
Springer-Verlag.
[41] Id. at 371–372.

standards). However, since the initial burst of interest and activity relating to MSIs, creation of new initiatives has slowed significantly and researchers have found that only a handful of new MSIs were launched during the 2010s. Other commentators have also noted that MSIs have gained wide support as "an umbrella framework for bringing together diverse constituencies to develop common approaches to contemporary global challenges and to present challenging development projects," but have pointed that each of the initiatives have a different configuration of corporations, governments, and civil society participants, a different procedure to set its terms of reference, and different sets of rules for making decisions and adopting policy statements.[42]

The developers of the Standards Map, which covers more than 250 MSIs applicable to more than 80 sectors and 180 countries, noted that some standards apply to a multitude of products or services, and cover numerous countries, while others are focused on a single product and a handful of countries. Standards may focus on one sustainability area, such as the environment, or may be more broad-based and attempt to cover multiple additional areas such as social issues, economic issues, ethics, and quality management. The participants in the development of standards will vary and can include international or regional public authorities, the private sector, civil society or by a consortium of public, private and civil society individuals.[43]

While many of the CSR-related initiatives are voluntary and thus do not fall within the ordinary governmental responsibilities with respect to interpretation and enforcement that apply to formal statutes and regulations, the government nonetheless has an obligation to participate in the CSR standards-setting processes in order to ensure that the standards support the orderly working of markets in a manner that is clear and fair for people and businesses. Governmental participation in the development of private CSR standards is also a good

---

[42] Gleckman, H. 2016. "Multi-Stakeholder Governance: A Corporate Push for a New Form of Global Governance. "In *State of Power 2016*, eds. N. Buxton and D. Eade. 91–93. Amsterdam: Transnational Institute.

[43] sustainabilitymap.org

way to confirm that those standards reflect agreed international norms and the principles of governmental agreements on labor, social, and environmental goals and standards. In addition, when governments can agree on the CSR standards that should apply to businesses that are operating within their borders, they can reduce confusion, promote standardized due diligence and monitoring practices, and create a "level playing field" across the globe that supports fair competition while protecting the rights of workers and local communities and preserving natural resources.[44]

Factors Driving the Emergence and Adoption of MSIs

Giovannucci et al. noted dramatic shifts in the business environment as vague concepts of sustainability and CSR began to be replaced by better defined and more transparent standards, including measurement and reporting, that consumers increasingly expected of the brands they chose.[45] Since governments, regardless of whether they could be trusted to do the job, were struggling to keep up with globalization and work together to develop a new legal framework for the relationship between business and social issues such as environmental protection and human rights, multinational corporations turned to voluntary standards. In fact, Giovannucci et al. pointed out that many firms sought to be "first movers" with respect to exploring and employing standards in order to capture the benefits of being able to establish a market position that appealed to the "heart space" of consumers and contributed to brand loyalty in unique ways.[46] Interestingly, some of the most innovative and effective standards initiatives have gone beyond the firm level to include

[44] "Overview of Selected Initiatives and Instruments Relevant to Corporate Social Responsibility." In Annual Report on the OECD Guidelines for Multinational Enterprises 2008 (Paris: Organisation for Economic Co-operation and Development, 2009), 235, 244.
[45] Giovannucci, D., O. von Hagen, and J. Wozniak. 2014. "Corporate Social Responsibility and the Role of Voluntary Sustainability Standards." In Voluntary Standards Systems, eds. C. Schmitz-Hoffmann et al., 359–363. Berlin: Springer-Verlag.
[46] Id.

industrywide collaborations to advance behavior by multiple firms in order to preempt governmental action and build goodwill among consumers and other interested stakeholders. Giovannucci et al. mentioned the Keystone Field to Market, SAI Platform, and Sustainable Food Labs as examples of platforms generated by the private sector based on a strategic opportunity approach to voluntary standards.[47]

A survey of 254 senior leaders in procurement and supply chain management conducted in 2010 looked at the key reasons for their interest in incorporating sustainability criteria into their functional processes. The results indicated that firms were driven by, in order of importance, economic reasons, customer demand, corporate mission/philosophy, reputation/public perception, limited resources, staff, regulatory requirements, and supplier requirements.[48]

According to Giovannucci et al., four recently emerging phenomena have been driving companies to adopt voluntary standards[49]:

- A *consumer environment* characterized by strong interest in personal health and concerns regarding the social and environmental conditions in the places where products originate;
- A concentrated and more competitive *business environment* requiring new methods of differentiation, more agile reputational risk management and more sophisticated supply chain management where greater efficiencies in costs and logistics are only the beginning;
- A *regulatory environment* with new and greater food safety requirements such as traceability and difficulties in keeping up with fast-moving global trade developments;
- Social *communications advances* that are global in scale, exposing corporations and individuals to greater levels of scrutiny that can alter reputations in a matter of hours and even offer tangible proof of civil or criminal responsibility regarding food safety, labor violations, and environmental impacts.

---

[47] Id. at 369.

[48] Id. at 369 (citing Roland Berger Strategy Consultants, BME-Bundesverband Materialwirtschaft, Einkaup und Logistik e. V. (2010), 370).

[49] Id. at 364–365.

A joint report prepared by the International Trade Centre and European University Institute in 2016 noted the increase in consumer demand for sustainable trade and the corresponding rise in the number and popularity of voluntary social and environmental standards (e.g., between 2008 and 2014, areas certified by the Roundtable on Sustainable Palm Oil increased almost thirtyfold and the Rainforest Alliance/Sustainable Agriculture Network's areas of coverage expanded more than ninefold. The report also acknowledged that global supply chains were another important driver of voluntary sustainability standards as lead firms came under pressure to ensure that the efficiency gains of those chains were not achieved at the expense of quality and safety. The report pointed out that multinational companies have turned to product and production process standards developed by the private sector as opposed to governments are that those standards are among several tools used to ensure that suppliers satisfy minimum quality, safety, social, and environmental norms.[50]

Assessments and Critiques of MSIs

As MSIs have proliferated, so have attempts to assess their contents and processes and make recommendations for improvements. For example, Chao noted that while there had been a proliferation of standard-setting initiatives, it remained unclear as to what extent those standards recognized and afforded protection for human rights. She and her colleagues, working with the support of a consortium of NGOs, invited representatives of six voluntary commodity standards schemes to engage in a comparative review of their standards to identify strengths and weaknesses and draw out key lessons for improvement and harmonization. The standards surveyed were those developed by the Roundtable on Sustainable Palm Oil, the Forest Stewardship Council, the Roundtable on Sustainable Biofuels, the Roundtable on Responsible Soy, the Shrimp Aquaculture Dialogue, and Bonsucro. Chao summarized the result of the

---

[50] *Social and Environmental Standards: Contributing to More Sustainable Value Chains*, iii. Geneva: ITC/EUI.

comparison of three important topics: customary land right; free, prior and informed consent; and rights to remedies.[51]

As to customary land rights, Chao explained that they were derived from traditional ownership, occupation, or other use in accordance with customary laws and customary practices, and had been afforded legal protections under international instruments (e.g., UN Declaration on the Rights of Indigenous Peoples (UNDRIP)), some national laws and, where formally recognized, under customary law. However, Chao noted that customary land rights had remained poorly protect across much of the Global South and that governments had continuously applied the principle of eminent domain to appropriate large swathes of land to investors while, as she put it, failing to give due consideration of the communities who maintained customary relations with those lands and depend on those lands directly for their livelihoods. The results of the survey confirmed that each of the standards required compliance with national and international laws, including in relation to land, and customary land users were generally acknowledged provided that there was no legitimate dispute over the land. However, only one of the standards explicitly mentioned food and water security, and where food, water, and land were mentioned they were generally treated in terms of access and management rather than as rights per se. The standards also failed to make distinctions among categories of land users (e.g., women, lower castes, migrant laborers, squatters, and nomadic pastoralists), each of which might have different rights and interests with respect to the land.

The right of free, prior, and informed consent (FPIC) is explicitly stated in the UNDRIP and implicitly integrated into a number of other human rights instruments. Chao explained that FPIC "is the right of indigenous peoples (and, in some cases, rural communities more generally) to give or to withhold their consent, through their self-chosen

---

[51] The discussion of Chao's article is adapted from S. Chao, Securing Human Rights through Private Sector Standards?, https://ourworld.unu.edu/en/securing-human-rights-through-private-sector-standards. See also the full study on the issues discussed in Chao's article: Chao, S., M. Colchester and N. Jiwan. 2012. *Securing Human Rights through Private Sector Standards? A Comparative Review.* Forest Peoples Programme and Rights and Resources Initiative.

representatives, to projects that may affect them and the resources upon which they depend." Chao noted that FPIC is most usefully understood as an expression of the right of all peoples to self-determination. Governments have a duty to protect FPIC and the standards should provide guidance as to how the consent process should work; however, while FPIC was explicitly stated in the principles and criteria of most of the surveyed standards, none of them explicitly stated that FPIC was tantamount to the right to withhold consent. Specific shortcomings in the standards included the failure to define what "informed consent" and "prior consent" meant in practice and the lack of requirements that consent be given without coercion. Several of the standards omitted any mention of the right of indigenous peoples to be represented by their own self-chosen representatives in interactions with a company or in the consent-seeking process. Other important questions that Chao and her colleagues felt had been left unanswered by the standards included:

- Who has the right to FPIC, and who has the legitimacy to represent communities in giving consent?
- How can elite co-optation be avoided?
- How informed do communities need to be, bearing in mind confidentiality clauses?
- When should the consent-seeking process start, and what are the relative roles of the government and of companies in seeking consent, especially where this is already an obligation of governments under international human rights law?

Chao noted that the right to remedies including restitution, compensation, rehabilitation, satisfaction, and guarantees or nonrepetition is not only a separately recognized right under international law, but also complements other recognized rights. Each of the standards included conflict resolution mechanisms and each of them required that disputes must be resolved prior to certification using the mechanism or a recognized form of mediation facility. However, Chao and her colleagues argued that there were shortcomings in the content and operation of the standards with respect to remedies: lack of clarity as to how a "conflict" is defined and what constitutes "resolution"; no requirement that companies suspend activities until a conflict is resolved; no requirement that grieved parties or local communities must participate in the development of conflict resolution mechanisms; no provisions for situations where a company's activities cause horizontal conflict across communities, as opposed to vertical conflict between the company and communities; and a preference for monetary compensation, often on disadvantageous terms to grieved parties, rather than land restitution.

In spite of the afore-described shortcomings, Chao praised the emergence of voluntary standards as an encouraging sign that businesses acknowledge that the rights of communities should be taken into account as development projects proceed and international human rights laws need to be considered even in situations where local laws are silent or ambiguous. However, standards have evolved separately and the resulting lack of harmonization has continued to create confusion, as well as opportunities for businesses to shirk their responsibilities. Chao emphasized the importance of community participation in the development of standards and the need to provide support to communities by building their capacities (e.g., technical know-how and access) to actually use the standards. This type of support has come from international human rights organizations, which have also played an important role in monitor private sector compliance with the standards and encouraging business to engage with the standards.

While standards such as the ones that were included in the survey described previously are often primarily focused on actions that can and should be taken by governments to affirmatively protect human rights, businesses cannot simply cede the field to the state and ignore the ethical, legal, and economic reasons for acting in a manner that demonstrates respect for human rights when make decisions relating to operational activities, such as embarking on development projects that will impact communities that lack the resources to understand and defend their rights. Voluntary standards, done well thoughtfully and well, can provide a good and recognized starting point for businesses; however, when necessary businesses should be prepared to voluntarily build on those standards and address some of the issues that have been mentioned previously. In effect, this means "going beyond both the law and minimum voluntary standards." For example, businesses should be wary of relying on governmental claims that eminent domain takings have been done in a manner consistent with due process and should be mindful that their proposed usage of lands should be analyzed not only for the impact on those dwelling on the lands but also those who rely on access to the lands for food and water. As for the rights of indigenous peoples, businesses can and should address the questions posed earlier by designing, in conjunction with community leaders, a fair consent-seeking process, even when local governments have failed to do the same. Finally, the rules for conflict resolution should be clear decisions regarding remedies should not be deferred until a project is done.

The Duke Human Rights Center at the Kenan Institute for Ethics and MSI Integrity carefully analyzed key attributes of 45 MSIs that set standards, govern corporate or government conduct and have transnational reach, looking at fundamental features of each MSI's scope, governance, and implementation structures including the types of stakeholders included in the initiatives and whether the initiatives monitored members for compliance with their standards. The sponsors acknowledged that their database examined only a handful of characteristics for each initiative; however, they argued that the following key findings provided important insights into the evolution of MSIs and how well they were doing in their efforts to close the governance gap referred to earlier[52]:

- MSIs appear to be creating an uneven patchwork of industry-specific standards that are largely clustered in a handful of industries, particularly consumer goods; agriculture, forestry, and fishing; and mining and energy. In fact, the sponsors found no industry-specific initiatives for finance, health care, or telecommunications.

---

[52] The New Regulators? Assessing the Landscape of Multi-Stakeholder Initiatives: Findings from a database of transnational standard-setting multi-stakeholder initiatives (MSI Integrity and the Duke Human Rights Center at the Kenan Institute for Ethics, June 2017), 3.

- The overwhelming majority of MSIs were failing to meaningfully engage communities affected by the operations of participating companies in either MSI governance or implementation. For example, only 14 percent of the surveyed MSIs reported that they involved any members of communities or other populations affected by MSI member companies in their primary decision-making body, and only 49 percent of the surveyed MSIs involved their affected communities in any of their activities or implementation at all.
- Almost half of the surveyed MSIs over-represented a single stakeholder group on their primary decision-making body. For example, 40 percent of the surveyed MSIs had governing bodies on which representatives from a single stakeholder group, such as companies or civil society, exceeded the number of stakeholders from any other group by a ratio of 2:1 or greater.
- Many of the surveyed MSIs did not have the mechanisms necessary to hold members to account if they breach MSI standards (e.g., suspension or expulsion from the initiative) and only 40 percent of the surveyed MSIs had any form of complaints process that would allow communities or individuals to report instances of human rights or environmental abuse that violated the initiative's standards.

MSIs have achieved varying levels of success and should certainly be lauded for their contributions to global governance and their roles as platforms for multistakeholder cooperation, dialogue and exchange of information. However, the findings outlined previously indicate that while MSIs have become and remain important, particularly in certain industries, future developers of new MSIs must address certain fundamental flaws common among existing MSIs including ensuring that the intended beneficiaries of the initiatives (e.g., workers, local communities, or indigenous groups) have meaning opportunities to shape the initiative's implementation and decision making and setting and enforcing compliance standards that are robust and reliable and provide protections to beneficiaries that are on par with traditional governance mechanisms interpreted and enforced by governments.[53]

In addition to the aforementioned issues, a review of critiques of MSIs and their potential to serve as a foundation for a new global governance framework by Gleckman led him to identify the following eight "cutting edge issues and concerns"[54]:

- *How are the categories of actors selected or excluded?* Designation of the key actors for any MSI can be ambiguous and choices must be made from a wide range of potential participants including governments (at the national, regional, and municipal levels), CSOs (at the international, regional and national levels), academics, gender-based or other rights groups, investors, manufacturing and servicing firms of various sizes, indigenous peoples, labor organizations, and other nonstate actors relevant in some way to the issue to be addressed by the MSI (e.g., educators, senior citizens, or nearby residents and communities). Gleckman argued that the selection process often tended to be biased toward those with an explicit stake in the outcome and other categories of stakeholder who are likely to agree with the approach of the sponsors of the MSI, thus excluding actors that might not be as cooperative with the sponsors or that will be negatively affected by the likely outcome of the MSI process.
- *How do the initiatives address the inherent power balance between actors?* Gleckman reminded that all categories of actors in any MSI are not created equal and that there are stark differences among them with respect to key characteristics such as the capacity to finance their participation in the MSI, ways to negotiate, technical skills and capacities to implement, or hinder the outcome of the MSI process.

---

[53] Id.
[54] Gleckman, H. 2016. "Multi-Stakeholder Governance: A Corporate Push for a New Form of Global Governance." In State of Power 2016. eds. N. Buxton and D. Eade, 91, 98–103. Amsterdam: Transnational Institute.

He argued that it was not sufficient to balance participation in an MSI based on geographic, gender, and relative political power grounds, but that consideration also needed to be given to strengthening access-to-resources-to-participate-effectively across the overall participation in the MSI and cautioned that it would likely take decades, as it did with the development of the existing multilateral system of nation-states illustrated by the UN, to devise credible ways to balance inherent resource and power differences between categories of actors in an MSI.

- *Who selects the organizations and individuals to represent each participant category?* While there are clear rules for how governments designate individuals to represent them in multilateral governmental bodies such as the UN, there is little consensus as to who is to have the authority to select or approve individual organizations, businesses, and institutions to fill the seats for each category of actors in an MSI. According to Gleckman, representatives of the actors in an MSI were seldom, if ever, designated by their corporate board, an NGO board of directors, or university trustees to act on behalf of that institution, but rather were usually selected on an informal one-to-one basis by the sponsoring organization.

- *What are the correct standards—or should there be standards—to select appropriate institutional participants for each category?* Consideration should be given to identifying and defining certain minimum standards for participants in the MSI process to ensure that they are proper and legitimate organizations. Gleckman suggested that selection standards could be derived from the criteria that multinational corporations now routinely use in their supply contracts, due diligence for mergers and risk assessments for business partners including verification that an organization works in conformity with the UN Charter and with widely accepted UN principles (such as the Universal Declaration of Human Rights and the Sustainable Development Goals [SDGs]).

- *What are the de facto terms of reference for the group?* Gleckman noted that the first step in the political processes that play out at the UN and in other multilateral bodies is often lengthy discussions and drafting to frame the issue to be addressed in the process. While MSIs must also define their problems and scopes, Gleckman suggested that they should take the lead, in advance of global political debates, in defining an issue and framing it in a way that a market-based solution is likely to be the "best" outcome.

- *Where does the cash involved come from and go to?* Consideration should be given to which institutions or participants are providing the tangible and intangible resources (e.g., direct payments, institutional resources, loaned organizational capacities, and money management) to finance and otherwise support the group and which institutions or participants are expected to provide the same types of resources to implement its recommendations. At a minimum, the group needs to be transparent about resource management and follow best practices regarding accounting. However, the potential impact of disproportionate resources on the outcomes of the process need to be considered, although the impact will vary depending on the balance between internally generated resources (e.g., what wealthier participants will want to fund) and externally supplied resources (e.g., support from government agencies, foundations, or corporate underwriting) used to support the MSI.

- *What is the internal decision-making process for the MSI?* As opposed to the multilateral system, which has painstakingly created its own well-developed rules on voting procedures, on how smaller or weaker nations can engage in issues with a sense of equity and even on resolving procedural disputes, there are no recognized standards governing the internal decision-making processes of MSIs and little in the way of guidelines that would clarify the obligations, responsibilities, and liabilities of MSI participants. One of the many issues that needs to be considered is the level of internal confidentiality with respect to agendas and discussions prior to public announcements on the status of the MSI process.

- *What are its external obligations?* While the outcome of multilateral negotiations includes clear instructions to participants (i.e., nation-states) regarding the expectations of them with respect to providing resources and other actions, there are no similar obligations for the participants in an MSI. Gleckman noted that not only is there an absence of obligations on participants to commit resources to implement the outcome of an MSI, there is also a lack of clarity on the way deliberations and outcomes are shared with the global public; the degree to which each governing actor is obliged to consult with the constituencies that it "represents," the opportunity the public have to challenge the MSI's proposals and the role the MSI might take in orchestrating government and other actors to implement its recommendations.

Gleckman echoed the views of others that governments, and the multilateral processes that they are familiar with, are no longer able to deal with the complex and unforeseen impacts of globalization and that it is time for a new system of multistakeholder governance that includes a broader range of other social groups, particularly those most adversely affected by globalization. He noted that it is not surprising that MNCs, which have achieved significant wealth and power during and as a result of globalization, are often taking the lead to establish themselves in crucial governance roles in this new system; however, governments and other stakeholders must proactively participate in the new system to ensure that their voices are heard in the drafting of new rules of engagement with MNCs. As for what the new system might look like, Gleckman's view is that there were several options including rebuilding the multilateral system so that it would also govern globalization and its economic, environmental, and social impacts; legally recognizing the de facto status that civil society and MNCs have in global decision making and designing a new global institution that incorporates an appropriate political balance between these sectors and supplants the existing government-based UN system; and adopting a new Vienna Convention specifying the rules for how MSIs could operate as an adjunct part of multilateralism.[55]

---

[55] Id. at 104–105.

Measuring the Impact of Standards

Giovannucci et al. noted that while there are a number of guidelines or frameworks for social accounting, environmental reporting, and even "auditing," relatively little is known about the actual impacts of voluntary standards, including their effects on productivity or risk, or how effective standards have been as a tool for furthering a firm's CSR objectives and initiatives. According to Giovannucci et al., the first attempts to assess standards tended to be in the form of very specific case studies of one point in time or anecdotal assessments. However, they were optimistic about the development of new tools for objective evaluation and understanding of voluntary standards such as International Trade Centre's Standards Map and the key indicators for measurement of social, economic, and environmental impacts developed by the Committee on Sustainability Assessment. In their opinion, the application of new information technology will facilitate the collection and analysis of comparable data regarding activities in complex global supply chains that can be verified and used to improve overall understanding of sustainability and the impact of voluntary standards.[56]

Recommendations for Improving MSIs

A joint report prepared by the International Trade Centre (ITC) and European University Institute in 2016 focused on uncovering factors making voluntary social and environmental standards more accessible to producers through cost sharing, assistance, and transparency and provided recommendations on how standard-setting organizations and value chain players could foster sustainable development and inclusiveness of small and medium enterprises (SMEs) and small farmers.[57] The Executive Summary to the report explained that the findings presented

---

[56] Giovannucci, D., O. von Hagen and J. Wozniak. 2014. "Corporate Social Responsibility and the Role of Voluntary Sustainability Standards." In *Voluntary Standards Systems*, eds. C. Schmitz-Hoffmann et al., 359, 373–375, and 382. Berlin: Springer-Verlag.

[57] *Social and Environmental Standards: Contributing to More Sustainable Value Chains*. Geneva: ITC/EUI, 2016.

in the report were based on the first econometric assessment of 181 voluntary sustainability standards sourced from ITC's Standards Map database. Among the highlights mentioned in the Executive Summary were the following[58]:

- Standards were growing, but not equally. Standards first emerged in developing countries, but a growing number of new standards were being created in developing countries, especially in large developing countries. Several standards had become truly global, and there was access to at least some voluntary certification opportunities in all countries. Standards covered goods, services, and processes, most frequently focusing on extraction and primary production.
- Stakeholder involvement, a crucial element in the governance of standards, varied significant with respect to range, types, and roles of stakeholders. The group with the highest level of engagement was producers, followed by civil society and buyers.
- Setters of sustainability standards supported producers in various ways, mostly through guidance tools and documents. Many of them also offered technical assistance in meeting the standards' requirements; however, little technical assistance was offered in other important areas such as improving productivity, efficiency, or market access. Many standard setters offered support to producers in developing countries to help them overcome capacity limitations, such as a lack of access to modern technologies, gaps in their technical knowledge of standards, or challenges in accessing finance.
- Transparency levels varied considerably across standards. Although almost all standard setters made information about standards' content available on their respective

---

websites, only one-third of the standards disclosed information about the certification/verification process and their application and development procedures. Transparency about assessment methodologies was even poorer. In general, more work was needed on ensuring that producers had access to essential information such as sustainability requirements, audit processes, standard setting, and development.

- The most frequent type of conformity assessment (i.e., the process of verifying whether a producer complies with the requirements of a standard) was third-party assessment conducted by independent certification or conformity assessment bodies.

- Demonstrating compliance with voluntary standards is becoming increasingly important for gaining access to value chains and consumer markets; however, the costs of compliance, which are often a fixed-cost component that is independent of the value of operations, can be daunting for SMEs and small farmers in developing countries. In 64 percent of the standards, producers were solely responsible for paying the implementation costs, and 28 percent of the standards used a model in which these costs are shared more equally between producers and other value chain actors. In only a very small proportion of cases were the implementation costs borne by the standards system (3 percent) or other value chain actors (4 percent), without any contribution from producers.

- Most standards had policies for labels and claims made in marketing material that could be used either directly on product packaging or off-product to demonstrate a producer's participation in a voluntary standard, thus allowing for differentiation of a producer's products from those of noncertified competitors.

- Traceability systems were employed by all of the voluntary standards to record and follow the production process, from farm through to the processing, packaging and distribution

stages, and ultimately to the stage where the product is
sold to the consumer. The most frequently used traceability
systems were systems involving "identity preservation,"
which required the strict separation of certified products
along the supply chain without mixing different certified
products.

The sponsors of the report noted that a key finding for standard setters
was that standards were less present in small countries and in countries
with weaker institutions and logistics, which the sponsors believed created opportunities for standard setters to help producers in these areas
overcome institutional challenges. The sponsors urged standards setters to increase standards availability; promote sharing of costs between
producers and other value chain actors; increase support to producers
and transparency in terms of sharing information on a standard's documents, standard-setting procedures, and certification and verification
decisions; and involve buyers and producers in standards at the board or
management level and adopt the International Social and Environmental
Accreditation and Labelling Principles.[59]

---

[59] Id. at xii.

CHAPTER 2

CSR Initiatives of Governmental or Intergovernmental Bodies

Many companies have looked to corporate social responsibility (CSR) initiatives of governmental or intergovernmental bodies as the foundation for creating their own CSR commitments. The instruments that have been developed and promoted by the United Nations and the other entities referenced below are widely recognized as legitimate standards that have emerged from a careful process of deliberation and input from a wide range of stakeholders with substantial experience in identifying problems and assessing potential solutions. In addition, several countries, including Canada, India, and a number of countries in the European Union, have developed CSR policies or guidance documents that outline their approach to CSR (see, e.g., National Strategy for Corporate Social Responsibility—Action Plan for CSR—of the German federal government).

OECD Guidelines for Multinational Enterprises

The OECD Guidelines for Multinational Enterprises (http://mneguidelines.oecd.org/) are the most comprehensive set of government-backed recommendations on responsible business conduct in existence today. The governments adhering to the Guidelines, all 36 OECD countries and 12 non-OECD countries, aim to encourage and maximize the positive impact multinational enterprises (MNEs) can make to sustainable development and enduring social progress. The Guidelines were first adopted in 1976 and have been reviewed five times since then to ensure that they remain a leading tool to promote responsible business conduct in the changing landscape of the global economy. The most recent update in 2011 took place with the active participation of business, labor, nongovernmental organizations (NGOs), nonadhering countries, and international organizations. The Guidelines are part of the OECD Declaration and Decisions on International Investment and Multinational Enterprises, and provide voluntary principles and standards for responsible business conduct by MNEs in areas such as employment and industrial relations, human rights, environment, information disclosure, combating bribery, consumer interests, science and technology, competition, and taxation.

Among other things, the Guidelines call for MNEs to take fully into account established policies in the countries in which they operate and consider the views of other stakeholders. In this regard, the General Policies in Section II of Part I of the Guidelines call for MNEs to:

- Contribute to economic, social, and environmental progress with a view to achieving sustainable development;
- Respect the human rights of those affected by their activities consistent with the host government's international obligations and commitments;
- Encourage local capacity building through close cooperation with the local community, including business interests, as well as developing the enterprise's activities in domestic and foreign markets, consistent with the need for sound commercial practice;
- Encourage human capital formation, in particular by creating employment opportunities and facilitating training opportunities for employees;
- Refrain from seeking or accepting exemptions not contemplated in the statutory or regulatory framework related to environmental, health, safety, labor, taxation, financial incentives, or other issues;
- Support and uphold good corporate governance principles and develop and apply good corporate governance practices;
- Develop and apply effective self-regulatory practices and management systems that foster a relationship of confidence

and mutual trust between enterprises and the societies in which they operate;

- Promote employee awareness of, and compliance with, company policies through appropriate dissemination of these policies, including through training programs;
- Refrain from discriminatory or disciplinary action against employees who make bona fide reports to management or, as appropriate, to the competent public authorities, on practices that contravene the law, the OECD Guidelines, or the enterprise's policies;
- Encourage, where practicable, business partners, including suppliers and subcontractors, to apply principles of corporate conduct compatible with the OECD Guidelines; and
- Abstain from any improper involvement in local political activities.

The Guidelines are voluntary; however, observance of the Guidelines by MNEs is generally expected and governments adhering to the Guidelines are required to set up a National Contact Point (NCP) whose main role is to further the effectiveness of the Guidelines by undertaking promotional activities, handling enquiries, and contributing to the resolution of issues that may arise from the alleged nonobservance of the guidelines in specific instances. NCPs assist enterprises and their stakeholders to take appropriate measures to further the observance of the Guidelines. They provide a mediation and conciliation platform for resolving practical issues that may arise with the implementation of the Guidelines.[1]

Implementation of the OECD Guidelines for Multinational Enterprises is promoted and facilitated by the OECD Due Diligence Guidance for Responsible Business Conduct, which was adopted in May 2018 to provide plain language explanations of due diligence recommendations and associated provisions in the Guidelines to help enterprises avoid and address adverse impacts related to workers, human rights, the environment, bribery, consumers, and corporate governance that may be

---

[1] www.oecd.org/investment/mne/ncps.htm

associated with their operations, supply chains, and other business relationships. Guidance tracks the various stages of the due diligence process, presented in a question-and-answer format, and should be consulted as a fundamental resource when developing due diligence policies and processes. The OECD has also issued several due diligence guidance publications focused on specific sectors including OECD Due Diligence Guidance for Responsible Supply Chains in the Garment and Footwear sector; OECD Due Diligence Guidance for Responsible Supply Chains of Minerals from Conflict-Affected and High-Risk Areas; OECD-FAO Guidance for Responsible Agricultural Supply Chains; and OECD guidance for institutional investors on implementing human rights due diligence.

G20/OECD Principles of Corporate Governance

Elements of CSR, including recognition of the rights of stakeholders along with shareholders and the need for regular and transparent reporting of the corporation's governance practices and performance, found their way into the G20/OECD Principles of Corporate Governance, which call on corporations to[2]:

- Distribute duties and responsibilities among different supervisory, regulatory and enforcement authorities;
- Protect and facilitate the exercise of shareholder rights and ensure equitable treatment of all shareholders, including minority and foreign shareholders;
- Recognize the rights of stakeholders established by law or through mutual agreements and ensure that where stakeholder interests are protected by law that stakeholders have the opportunity to obtain effective redress for violation of their rights;

---

[2] *Organisation for Economic Co-operation and Development, G20/OECD Principles of Corporate Governance* (Paris: OECD Publishing, 2015) http://dx.doi.org/10.1787/9789264236882-en

- Encourage active cooperation between corporations and stakeholders in creating wealth, jobs, and the sustainability of financially sound enterprises;
- Permit mechanisms for employee participation to develop;
- Ensure that stakeholders participating in the corporate governance process have access to relevant, sufficient, and reliable information on a timely and regular basis and are able to freely communicate their concerns about illegal or unethical practices to the board and to the competent public authorities without compromising their rights;
- Publish regular and accurate disclosure concerning the company's financial situation, performance, ownership, and governance that includes, among other things, company objectives and nonfinancial information in accordance with high-quality standards including policies and performance relating to business ethics, the environment, and, where material to the company, social issues, human rights and other public policy commitments; foreseeable risks factors including business conduct risks; and risks related to the environment; key issues relevant to employees and other stakeholders that may materially affect the performance of the company or that may have significant impacts upon them; and governance structures and policies, including the content of any corporate governance code or policy and the process by which it is implemented;
- Implement a corporate governance framework that ensures the strategic guidance of the company, the effective monitoring of management by the board, the board's accountability to the company and the shareholders and effective disclosures and communications to stakeholders; and
- Ensure that the board applies high ethical standards and takes into account the interests of stakeholders through the adoption, implementation, and enforcement of companywide codes of conduct that serve as a standard for conduct by both the board and key executives and set the framework for the exercise of judgment in dealing with varying and often conflicting constituencies.

International Labour Organization

The International Labour Organization (ILO) (www.ilo.org) is the only tripartite United Nations agency and brings together governments, employers, and workers representatives of 187 Member States, to set labor standards, develop policies, and devise programs promoting decent work for all women and men. Since 1919, the ILO has maintained and developed a system of international labor standards aimed at promoting opportunities for women and men to obtain decent and productive work, in conditions of freedom, equity, security, and dignity. Subjects covered by the standards include freedom of association, collective bargaining, forced and child labor, equality of opportunity and treatment, tripartite consultation, labor administration and inspection, employment policy, employment promotion, vocational guidance and training, employment security, wages, working time, occupational safety and health, social security, maternity protection, social policy, migrants workers, HIV/AIDS, seafarers and fishers, dock workers, indigenous and tribal peoples, and other specific categories of workers. International labor standards are addressed to ILO Member States, not to companies, and once a Convention or Declaration is ratified it is up to governments to implement and enforce through national legislation. However, companies may refer to a Convention or Declaration when establishing their CSR commitments and include in those commitments an undertaking to "give effect" to or "act in compliance with" the principles of the Convention or Declaration.[3]

Key ILO documents include the 2008 Declaration on Social Justice for a Fair Globalization, which expresses the universality of the Decent Work Agenda and calls for: all ILO members to pursue policies based on the strategic objectives that include employment, social protection, social dialogue, and rights at work; the 1998 Declaration on Fundamental Principles and Rights at Work, which commits ILO members to respect and promote principles and rights with respect to freedom of association and the effective recognition of the right to collective bargaining, the elimination of forced or compulsory labor, the abolition of

---

[3] *Handbook on Corporate Social Responsibility (CSR) for Employers' Organizations* (European Union CSR for All Project, April 2014), 33.

child labor, and the elimination of discrimination in respect of employment and occupation; and the Tripartite Declaration of Principles Concerning Multinational Enterprises and Social Policy (ILO MNE Declaration), which was first adopted by the ILO Governing Body in November 1977, updated in 2000 to incorporate the 1998 Declaration on Fundamental Principals and Rights at Work and further revised in 2006 and 2017.

The ILO MNE Declaration provides guidance to governments, employers' and workers' organizations, multinational enterprises, and national enterprises and is not mandatory, nor is it a code of conduct for business. Instead, it can be used as a reference for companies with respect to social policy and inclusive, responsible, and sustainable workplace practices. The ILO MNE Declaration sets out principles built on international labor standards in the areas of employment, training, conditions of work and life, and industrial relations as well as general policies. These include the fundamental principles and rights at work but also guidance on many other facets of decent work. The 2017 revisions were intended to respond to new economic realities, including increased international investment and trade, and the growth of global supply chains, and to take into account new labor standards adopted by the International Labour Conference, the Guiding Principles on Business and Human Rights endorsed by the Human Rights Council in 2011, and the 2030 Agenda for Sustainable Development. Specifically, new principles were added in 2017 to address decent work issues related to social security, forced labor, transition from the informal to the formal economy, wages, access to remedy, and compensation of victims. Guidance on "due diligence" processes was also added, consistent with the UN Guiding Principles on Business and Human Rights.[4]

The ILO also has a training arm, the International Training Centre (https://itcilo.org/en), which runs training, learning, and capacity development services for governments, employers' organizations, workers'

---

[4] ILO Revises Its Landmark Declaration on Multinational Enterprises (March 17, 2017), https://ilo.org/global/about-the-ilo/newsroom/news/WCMS_547615/lang—en/index.htm

organizations, and other national and international partners in support of decent work and sustainable development.

International Finance Corporation

The latest version of the International Finance Corporation (IFC) Performance Standards on Environmental and Social Sustainability went into effect on January 1, 2012. The IFC (www.ifc.org) has a Sustainability Framework that articulates the IFC's strategic commitment to sustainable development and is an integral part of IFC's approach to risk management. The Sustainability Framework comprises IFC's Policy and Performance Standards on Environmental and Social Sustainability, and IFC's Access to Information Policy. The Policy on Environmental and Social Sustainability describes IFC's commitments, roles, and responsibilities related to environmental and social sustainability. IFC's Access to Information Policy reflects IFC's commitment to transparency and good governance on its operations, and outlines the corporation's institutional disclosure obligations regarding its investment and advisory services.

The Performance Standards are directed toward clients, providing guidance on how to identify risks and impacts, and are designed to help avoid, mitigate, and manage risks and impacts as a way of doing business in a sustainable way, including stakeholder engagement and disclosure obligations of the client in relation to project-level activities. In the case of its direct investments (including project and corporate finance provided through financial intermediaries), IFC requires its clients to apply the Performance Standards to manage environmental and social risks and impacts so that development opportunities are enhanced. IFC uses the Sustainability Framework along with other strategies, policies, and initiatives to direct its business activities in order to achieve its overall development objectives. Together, the eight Performance Standards establish standards that the client is to meet throughout the life of an investment by IFC and cover: assessment and management of environmental and social risks and impacts; labor and working conditions; resource efficiency and pollution prevention; community health, safety, and security; land acquisition and involuntary resettlement; biodiversity conservation and sustainable management of living natural resources; indigenous peoples; and cultural heritage.[5]

The Performance Standards may also be applied by other financial institutions. For example, the Standards have been incorporated by private banks and other financial institutions into their assessment of project finance and project-related corporate loan proposals through their commitment to adhere to the Equator Principles (equator-principles.com), which is a risk management framework adopted by financial institutions for determining, assessing, and managing environmental and social risk in projects and is primarily intended to provide a minimum standard for due diligence and monitoring to support responsible risk decision making.

Principles for Responsible Investment

The Principles for Responsible Investment (www.unpri.org) calls itself the world's leading proponent of responsible investment and works to understand the investment implications of environmental, social, and governance (ESG) factors and to support its international network of investor signatories in integrating these factors into their investment and ownership decisions. The PRI is a nonprofit organization that engages with global policy makers but is not associated with any government; it is supported by, but not part of, the United Nations. The PRI defines "responsible investment" as an approach to investing that aims to incorporate ESG factors into investment decisions, to better manage risk and generate sustainable, long-term returns. Environmental factors include climate change, greenhouse gas emissions, resource depletion (including water), waste and pollution, and deforestation. Social factors include working conditions, including slavery and child labor; local communities, including indigenous communities; conflict; health and safety; and employee relations and diversity. Governance factors include executive pay, bribery, and corruption, political lobbying and donations, board diversity and structure, and tax strategy. Signatories agree to follow six principles: we will incorporate ESG issues into investment analysis and decision-making

---

[5] For further information see the "Performance Standards" page in the IFC website (www.ifc.org).

processes; we will be active owners and incorporate ESG issues into our ownership policies and practices; we will seek appropriate disclosure on ESG issues by the entities in which we invest; we will promote acceptance and implementation of the principles within the investment industry; we will work together to enhance our effectiveness in implementing the principles; and we will each report on our activities and progress toward implementing the principles.

United Nations Declaration on the Rights of Indigenous Peoples

The United Nations Declaration on the Rights of Indigenous Peoples (UNDRIP) was adopted, following over two decades of deliberation and debate, by a majority of the states in the UN General Assembly in September 2007 (Australia, Canada, New Zealand, and the United States were the four states that opposed the UNDRIP at that time; however, all four of them have since reversed the opposition, with the United States being the last to do so in December 2010). The UNDRIP is lengthy; however, the goal was to identify, describe, and affirm certain rights believed to be essential for preserve indigenous peoples' identity: the right to live in dignity and maintain and strengthen their own institutions, cultures, and traditions; the right to self-determination with respect to their economic, social, and cultural development in keeping with their own needs and aspirations; the right to participate in decision making; the right to lands, territories, and resources; and the right to culture.[6] Governments at all levels have struggled to implement the duties of states laid out in the UNDRIP with respect to free, prior, and informed consent, which calls on states to consult with indigenous peoples on legislative and administrative measures affecting them, such as forced relocation, culture, intellectual property, lands, territories, and resources, as well as development planning within the state, with a view to obtaining indigenous peoples' free, prior, and informed consent. For example, the United States, when it finally endorsed the UNDRIP, noted that while it understood the importance of a call for a process of meaningful consultation with tribal

---

[6] http://un.org/esa/socdev/unpfii/documents/faq_drips_en.pdf

leaders, it did not necessarily endorse and accept the notion that agreement of those leaders must be obtained before the actions addressed in those consultations are taken. Clearly companies need to tread carefully and deliberately when considering investment and development projects that will impact indigenous peoples in their communities and must be sure to understand and adhere to any formal legal standards and establish a process on their own that meets or exceeds best practices for CSR.[7]

United Nations Global Compact

The United Nations Global Compact (https://unglobalcompact.org/), often referred to simply as the "Global Compact," is a voluntary initiative launched in 1999 under the inspiration of former UN Secretary-General Kofi Annan that is based on CEO commitments to implement universal sustainability principles and to take steps to support United Nations goals. By encouraging companies to operate responsibly and take strategic actions that support society, the Global Compact works to ensure that business activity adds value not only to the bottom-line, but also to people, communities, and the planet. At the same time, businesses can help to improve the social and environmental framework that is necessary in order for them to have continued access to the open and free markets needed for their economic success. The Global Compact is based on the proposition that companies should take a comprehensive approach to sustainability and must operate responsibly in alignment with universal principles, take strategic actions that support the society around them, commit to sustainability at the highest level, report annually on their efforts, and engage locally where they have a presence.

The Global Compact encompasses ten principles that were derived from standards in four areas: human rights (the Universal Declaration of Human Rights, labor (the International Labour Organization's Declaration on Fundamental Principles and Rights at Work), the environment (the Rio Declaration on Environment and Development), and

---

[7] For further discussion, see Lewis, C. 2012. *Corporate Responsibility to Respect the Rights of Minorities and Indigenous Peoples.* Minority Rights Group International.

corruption (the United Nations Convention Against Corruption). These ten principles are as follows:

Human Rights
Principle 1: Businesses should support and respect the protection of internationally proclaimed human rights; and
Principle 2: make sure that they are not complicit in human rights abuses.

Labor
Principle 3: Businesses should uphold the freedom of association and the effective recognition of the right to collective bargaining;
Principle 4: the elimination of all forms of forced and compulsory labor;
Principle 5: the effective abolition of child labor; and
Principle 6: the elimination of discrimination in respect of employment and occupation.

Environment
Principle 7: Businesses should support a precautionary approach to environmental challenges;
Principle 8: undertake initiatives to promote greater environmental responsibility; and
Principle 9: encourage the development and diffusion of environmentally friendly technologies.

Anticorruption
Principle 10: Businesses should work against corruption in all its forms, including extortion and bribery.

A European Union publication has explained that the Global Compact is not a legal instrument; it is aspirational, and that companies who become signatories to the Global Compact do so in order to make a public commitment that they are prepared to work toward the achievement of the Global Compact's objectives by making the ten principles an integral part of their business strategies and day-to-day operations.

Signatories to the Global Compact have opportunities to engage in the exchange of information on initiatives undertaken in the course of the promotion of the principles, thus allowing the Global Compact to serve as a "learning model." Signatories can also develop networks at regional, national, and sectoral levels to engage in dialogue, learning, and projects that suit local contexts. However, being a signatory to the Global Compact requires accountability and signatories must commit to issuing an annual Communication on Progress (COP), which is a public disclosure to stakeholders (e.g., investors, consumers, civil society, governments, etc.) on progress made in implementing the ten principles, and in supporting broader UN development goals. If a signatory fails to communicate its progress by the deadline, it will be listed as "non-communicating" on the UN Global Compact website. If a further year passes without the submission of a COP, the company will be expelled. The Compact reserves the right to publish the names of companies that have been expelled for failure to comply with this requirement.[8]

As of June 2020, there were over 10,800 signatories to the Global Compact in 156 countries, both developed and developing, representing nearly every sector and size, making it the world's most popular multistakeholder CSR initiative. While businesses were and remain the primary focus of the initiative, the Global Compact, which has its offices in New York, has attracted support and involvement from a variety of nonbusiness participants including trade unions and a number of human rights and environmental NGOs that are willing and able to bring their expertise and experience to the Global Compact, enhance its learning focus and thereby enhance the development of good practices.[9]

United Nations Human Rights Instruments

The term "human rights" was mentioned seven times in the United Nation's founding Charter, making the promotion and protection of human rights a key purpose and guiding principle of the Organization.

---

[8] *Handbook on Corporate Social Responsibility (CSR) for Employers' Organizations* (European Union CSR for All Project, April 2014), 17–18.
[9] Id.

The Office of the UN High Commissioner for Human Rights (OHCHR) (http://ohchr.org/) has led responsibility in the UN system for the promotion and protection of human rights and supports the human rights components of peacekeeping missions in several countries, and has many country and regional offices and centers. The Human Rights Council, established in 2006, replaced the 60-year-old UN Commission on Human Rights as the key independent UN intergovernmental body responsible for human rights. The Universal Declaration of Human Rights (1948) was the first legal document protecting universal human rights. Together with the International Covenant on Civil and Political Rights and the International Covenant on Economic, Social and Cultural Rights, the three instruments form the so-called International Bill of Human Rights.

A series of international human rights treaties and other instruments that have been adopted since 1945 have expanded the body of international human rights law. Of note for business enterprises are the "Guiding Principles on Business and Human Rights: Implementing the United Nations 'Protect, Respect and Remedy' Framework" ("Guiding Principles"), which were developed by the Special Representative of the Secretary-General on the issue of human rights and transnational corporations and other business enterprises after extensive consultation and were endorsed by the Human Rights Council in its resolution 17/4 of June 16, 2011. The Guiding Principles were not intended to impose new legal obligations on business, or change the nature of existing human rights instruments, instead their aim is to articulate what these established instruments mean, for both States and companies, and to address the gap between law and practice.[10] Since they were first approved the Guiding Principles have become the global standard for the respective roles and duties of states and businesses relative to human rights and have been integrated as central elements of other well-known international standards such as the OECD Guidelines for Multinational Enterprises and IFC Performance Standards and ISO 26000 Social Responsibility Guidance.

---

[10] *Handbook on Corporate Social Responsibility (CSR) for Employers' Organizations* (European Union CSR for All Project, April 2014), 18.

The Guiding Principles are organized into three parts, each of which represents an important general principle underlying the "protect-respect-remedy" framework that was endorsed by the UN Human Rights Council in 2008:

- All states have existing obligations to respect, protect, and fulfill human rights and fundamental freedoms
- Business enterprises, both transnational and others, regardless of their size, sector, location, ownership, and structure, have a role as specialized organs of society performing specialized functions and are required to comply with all applicable laws and to respect human rights
- The need for rights and obligations to be matched to appropriate and effective remedies when breached.[11]

The introduction to the Guiding Principles made it clear that they should be implemented in a nondiscriminatory manner, with particular attention to the rights and needs of, as well as the challenges faced by, individuals from groups or populations that may be at heightened risk of becoming vulnerable or marginalized, and with due regard to the different risks that may be faced by women and men.

The Guiding Principles begin by focusing on the duties of states to protect against human rights abuse within their territory and/or jurisdiction by third parties, including business enterprises, through appropriate steps to prevent, investigate, punish, and redress such abuse through effective policies, legislation, regulations, and adjudication. With regard to business enterprises, states are expected to clearly set out expectations that all business enterprises domiciled in their territory and/or jurisdiction respect human rights throughout their operations and take additional steps in situations where activities of the state intersect with business (e.g., guarding against human rights abuses by business enterprises that are owned or

---

[11] The description of the Guiding Principles that follows is adapted from Guiding Principles on Business and Human Rights: Implementing the United Nations 'Protect, Respect and Remedy' Framework (United Nations Human Rights Office of the High Commissioner, HR/PUB/11/04, 2011).

controlled by the state, or that receive substantial support and services from state; and promoting respect for human rights by business enterprises with which they conduct commercial transactions). States are also expected to provide governmental departments, agencies, and other state-based institutions that shape business practices with relevant information, training, and support to ensure they are aware of and observe the state's human rights obligations when fulfilling their respective mandates. The Guiding Principles also include specific duties and obligations on states with respect to ensuring, through judicial, administrative, legislative, or other appropriate means, that when human rights abuses occur within their territory and/or jurisdiction those affected have access to effective remedies including effective domestic judicial and nonjudicial grievance mechanisms.[12]

As for business enterprises, the Guiding Principles are clear about their responsibilities to respect all internationally recognized human rights including, at a minimum, as those expressed in the International Bill of Human Rights and the principles concerning fundamental rights set out in the International Labour Organization's Declaration on Fundamental Principles and Rights at Work.[13] The responsibility to respect human rights requires that business enterprises avoid causing or contributing to adverse human rights impacts through their own activities, and address such impacts when they occur; and seek to prevent or mitigate adverse human rights impacts that are directly linked to their operations, products or services by their business relationships, even if

---

[12] While the Guiding Principles emphasize the role of the state in ensuring effective remedies for victims of human rights abuses, the Guiding Principles also look to industry, multistakeholder, and other collaborative initiatives to support the availability of effective grievance mechanisms (see Guiding Principle 30).

[13] The Commentary to Guiding Principle 12 notes that depending on circumstances, business enterprises may need to consider additional standards applicable to specific groups or populations that require particular attention, where they may have adverse human rights impacts on them (e.g., United Nations instruments on the rights of indigenous peoples; women; national or ethnic, religious and linguistic minorities; children; persons with disabilities; and migrant workers and their families), and standards of international humanitarian law in situations of armed conflicts.

they have not contributed to those impacts. In order to meet their responsibility to respect human rights, business enterprises should have in place policies and processes appropriate to their size and circumstances, including a policy commitment to meet their responsibility to respect human rights; a human rights due diligence process to identify, prevent, mitigate, and account for how they address their impacts on human rights; and processes to enable the remediation of any adverse human rights impacts they cause or to which they contribute.

While the Guiding Principles do not impose enforcement responsibilities with respect to human rights on businesses, they are expected to engage in ongoing reviews of their activities and relationships to ensure that they are not adversely impacting human rights and consult with all affected groups, disseminate their findings, remedy any direct or indirect violations, and monitor the effectiveness of remedial measures to confirm that all issues have been addressed.[14] The Guiding Principles do not require that businesses actively "promote" or advance human rights; however, companies interested in taking on those types of responsibilities may do so by committing to follow the Global Compact and/or conduct their operations in a manner that is consistent with pursuit of the UN's Sustainable Development Goals discussed below. In fact, businesses often promote human rights through community investment projects, such as building schools and cultural centers, but such actions cannot be used to offset negative human rights impacts from other aspects of the company's operations.

United Nations Sustainable Development Goals

The 17 Sustainable Development Goals (SDGs) of the 2030 Agenda for Sustainable Development were adopted by world leaders in September 2015 and went into effect on January 1, 2016. It was intended that over the fifteen-year period running through 2030 the SDGs, and their accompanying 169 targets, would be universally applied to all and

---

[14] Sharom, A., J. Purnama, M. Mullen, M. Asuncion, and M. Hayes, eds. 2018. *An Introduction to Human Rights in Southeast Asia*, Vol 1, 171–174. Nakhorn Pathom, Thailand: Southeast Asian Human Rights Studies Network.

that countries would mobilize efforts to end all forms of poverty, fight inequalities, and tackle climate change, while ensuring that no one is left behind. The UN website for the SDGs explained:

> The SDGs, also known as Global Goals, build on the success of the Millennium Development Goals (MDGs) and aim to go further to end all forms of poverty. The new Goals are unique in that they call for action by all countries, poor, rich, and middle-income to promote prosperity while protecting the planet. They recognize that ending poverty must go hand-in-hand with strategies that build economic growth and addresses a range of social needs including education, health, social protection, and job opportunities, while tackling climate change and environmental protection.[15]

While the SDGs are not legally binding, it is intended that national governments will be expected to take ownership and establish national frameworks for the achievement of the 17 SDGs and that countries will have the primary responsibility for follow-up and review of the progress made in implementing the SDGs. Provisions have also been made for monitoring and review of the SDGs using a set of global indicators developed by the UN Statistical Commission and adopted by the Economic and Social Council and the UN General Assembly will then adopt these indicators. The following is a brief summary of each of the SDGs[16]:

> *Goal 1—No Poverty: End* poverty in all its forms, everywhere. Poverty is to be broadly construed to include not only lack of income or resources, but also the lack of basic services, such as education, hunger, social discrimination, and exclusion, and the inability to meaningfully participate in decision making. Gender

---

[15] http://un.org/sustainabledevelopment/sustainable-development-goals/

[16] Sources for the discussion of the Goals include http://un.org/sustainable development/sustainable-development-goals/ and https://en.wikipedia.org/wiki/Sustainable_Development_Goals

inequality plays a major role in the perpetuation of poverty and its associated risks, since many women face life-threatening risks from early pregnancies and then continue to struggle with little or no hope of getting an education that could lead to a better income.

Goal 2—Zero Hunger: End hunger, achieve food security, and improved nutrition and promote sustainable agriculture. Under-nourishment and poor nutrition are serious risks in many parts of the world and agriculture remains the single largest employer in the world. Targets for this goal include ending hunger and ensuring access by all people, in particular the poor and people in vulnerable situations, including infants, to safe, nutritious, and sufficient food all year round; ending all forms of malnutrition; improving agricultural productivity and the incomes of small-scale food producers; ensuring sustainable food production systems and implementing resilient agricultural practices; maintaining the genetic diversity of seeds; increasing investment in rural infrastructure; and correcting and preventing trade restrictions and distortions in world agricultural markets and ensuring the proper functioning of food commodity markets.

Goal 3—Good Health and Well-being: Ensuring healthy lives and promoting well-being for all at all ages. Issues of concern for this goal include reducing the global maternal mortality ratio; ending preventable deaths of newborns and children under five years of age; end epidemics of AIDS, tuberculosis, malaria, and neglected tropical diseases and combat hepatitis, water-borne diseases and other communicable diseases; reducing premature mortality from noncommunicable diseases through prevention and treatment; strengthening the prevention and treatment of substance abuse; drastically reducing the number of global death and injuries from road traffic accidents; ensuring universal access to sexual and reproductive health care services, including for family planning, information, and education; achieving universal health coverage; and substantially reducing the number of deaths and illnesses from hazardous chemicals and air, water and soil pollution and contamination.

Goal 4—Quality Education: Ensure inclusive and equitable quality education and promote lifelong learning opportunities for all. The key target for this goal is ensuring that all girls and boys complete free, equitable, and quality primary and secondary education leading to relevant and effective learning outcomes.

Goal 5—Gender Equality: Achieve gender equality and empower all women and girls. The focus of this goal is on providing women and girls with equal access to education, health care, decent work, and representation in political and economic decision-making processes in order to fuel sustainable economies and benefit societies and humanity at large. In many countries, gender discrimination remains difficult to overcome due to legal and social norms, a situation that makes it much more challenging to achieve the other social development goals. Targets for this goal include not only adopting and strengthening sound policies and enforceable legislation for the promotion of gender equality and empowerment of all women and girls but also eliminating violence such as trafficking and sexual exploitation, mandating compulsory completion of secondary education for girls, implementation and accessibility of sexual and reproductive health rights to women and girls globally, aiding and empowering women and girls through technology and consultation with women and girls about their needs.

Goal 6—Clean Water and Sanitation: Ensure availability and sustainable management of water and sanitation for all. Among the targets for this goal are achieving universal and equitable access to safe and affordable drinking water for all; achieving access to adequate and equitable sanitation and hygiene for all; and improving water quality by reducing pollution, eliminating dumping and minimizing release of hazardous chemicals and materials; and substantially increasing recycling and safe reuse globally. Progress with respect to this goal is considered essential to achieving a number of the other goals including sustainable consumption and production, zero hunger, sustainable cities, and communities, no poverty and decent work and economic growth.

Goal 7—Affordable and Clean Energy: Ensure access to affordable, reliable, sustainable, and modern energy for all. Targets other than universal access for this goal include increasing substantially the share of renewable energy in the global energy mix; doubling the global rate of improvement in energy efficiency; and expanding infrastructure and upgrade technology for supplying modern and sustainable energy services for all in developing countries.

Goal 8—Decent Work and Economic Growth: Promote sustained, inclusive, and sustainable economic growth, full and productive employment and decent work for all. The targets associated with this goal are extensive and diverse and include sustaining per capita economic growth in accordance with national circumstances; achieving higher and, in particular, at least 7 percent gross domestic product growth per annum in the least developed countries; achieving higher levels of economic productivity through diversification, technological upgrading, and innovation; improving global resource efficiency in consumption and production; achieving full and productive employment and decent work for all women and men; substantially reducing the proportion of youth not in employment, education, or training; taking immediate and effective measures to eradicate forced labor and end modern slavery and human trafficking; and various measures relating to training of youth and reducing youth unemployment.

Goal 9—Industry, Innovation, and Infrastructure: Build resilient infrastructure, promote inclusive and sustainable industrialization, and foster innovation. Targets for this goal include developing quality, reliable, sustainable, and resilient infrastructure; promoting inclusive and sustainable industrialization; increasing the access of small-scale industrial and other enterprises, in particular in developing countries, to financial services, including affordable credit, and their integration into value chains and markets; upgrading infrastructure and retrofit industries to make them sustainable, with increased resource-use efficiency and greater adoption of clean and environmentally sound technologies and industrial processes; enhancing scientific research; facilitating sustainable and resilient infrastructure development in developing countries; supporting domestic technology development, research, and innovation in developing countries; and significantly increasing access to information and communications technology and striving to provide universal and affordable access to the Internet in least developed countries.

Goal 10—Reduced Inequalities: Reduce income inequality within and among countries. Targets for this goal include progressively achieving and sustaining income growth of the bottom 40 percent of the population at a rate higher than the national average; empowering and promoting the social, economic, and political inclusion of all, irrespective of age, sex, disability, race, ethnicity, origin, religion, or economic or other status; ensuring equal opportunity and reduce inequalities of outcome, including by eliminating discriminatory laws, policies, and practices and promoting appropriate legislation, policies, and action in this regard; adopting policies, especially fiscal, wage and social protection policies, and progressively achieve greater equality; improving the regulation and monitoring of global financial markets and institutions and strengthening the implementation of such regulations; and ensuring enhanced representation and voice for developing countries in decision making in global international economic and financial institutions in order to deliver more effective, credible, accountable, and legitimate institutions.

Goal 11—Sustainable Cities and Communities: Make cities and human settlements inclusive, safe, resilient, and sustainable. Targets for this goal include ensuring access for all to adequate, safe, and affordable housing and basic services and upgrade slums; providing access to safe, affordable, accessible, and sustainable transport systems for all and improving road safety; enhancing inclusive and sustainable urbanization and capacity for participatory, integrated, and sustainable human settlement planning and management in all countries; strengthen efforts to protect and safeguard the world's cultural and natural heritage; significantly reducing the number of deaths and the number of people affected and substantially decrease the direct economic losses relative to global gross domestic product caused by disasters, including water-related disasters; reducing the adverse per capita environmental impact of cities; and providing universal access to safe, inclusive, and accessible, green and public spaces, in particular for women and children, older persons, and persons with disabilities.

Goal 12—Responsible Consumption and Production: Ensure sustainable consumption and production patterns. Targets for this goal include implementing a framework of programs on sustainable consumption; achieving the sustainable management and efficient use of natural resources; substantially reducing per capita global food waste at the retail and consumer levels and reduce food losses along production and supply chains, including post-harvest losses; achieving the environmentally sound management of chemicals and all wastes throughout their life cycle; substantially reducing waste generation through prevention, reduction, recycling, and reuse; and ensuring that people everywhere have the relevant information and awareness for sustainable development and lifestyles in harmony with nature.

Goal 13—Climate Action: Take urgent action to combat climate change and its impacts by regulating emissions and promoting developments in renewable energy. Targets for this goal include strengthening resilience and adaptive capacity to climate-related hazards and natural disasters in all countries; integrating climate change measures into national policies, strategies and planning; improving education, awareness-raising and human and institutional capacity on climate change mitigation, adaptation, impact reduction, and early warning; and implementing the commitments undertaken by the parties to the United Nations Framework Convention on Climate Change.

Goal 14—Life Below Water: Conserve and sustainably use the oceans, seas, and marine resources for sustainable development. The targets associated with this goal include preventing and reducing marine pollution of all kinds; achieving and maintaining sustainable management and protection of the marine and costal ecosystem; minimizing acidification of the oceans; regulating overfishing; and increasing scientific knowledge on the area.

Goal 15—Life on Land: Protect, restore, and promote sustainable use of terrestrial ecosystems, sustainably manage forests, combat desertification, and halt and reverse land degradation and halt biodiversity loss. There are numerous targets for this goals including ensuring the conservation, restoration, and sustainable use of terrestrial and inland freshwater ecosystems and their services, in particular forests, wetlands, mountains, and drylands, in line with obligations under international agreements; promoting the implementation of sustainable management of all types of forests, halting deforestation, restoring degraded forests, and substantially increasing afforestation and reforestation globally; and combating desertification, restoring degraded land and soil, including land affected by desertification, drought and floods, and striving to achieve a land degradation-neutral world.

Goal 16—Peace, Justice, and Strong Institutions: Promote peaceful and inclusive societies for sustainable development, provide access to justice for all and build effective, accountable, and inclusive institutions at all levels. Targets for this goal include significantly reducing all forms of violence and related death rates everywhere; ending abuse, exploitation, trafficking, and all forms of violence against and torture of children; promoting the rule of law at the national and international levels and ensure equal access to justice for all; substantially reducing corruption and bribery in all their forms; and developing effective, accountable, and transparent institutions at all levels.

Goal 17—Partnerships for the Goals: Strengthen the means of implementation and revitalize the global partnership for sustainable development. Targets for these goals a largely at the country level and cover a number of areas including finance, technology, capacity building, trade, policy, and institutional coherence, multistakeholder partnerships and data, monitoring, and accountability.

While it is expected that national governments would take the lead in efforts to pursue and achieve global progress with respect to the SDGs, the SDGs are often incorporated into the sustainability-related mission and objectives of individual businesses and other organizations. This is especially true with respect to the activities undertaken in the local communities where the organizations operate since this is the level at which organizations have the best opportunity to make an impact through their community involvement and investment programs. Delivery of the SDGs in the 2030 Agenda for Sustainable Development should be important to businesses that realize that they will not be able to achieve sustainable success in a world of poverty, inequality, unrest, and environmental stress. As such, it has been argued that companies should contribute to the SDGs not just by "doing good," but also by upholding recognized standards and principles on human rights, labor, the environment, and anticorruption and transparently reporting on their SDG-related priorities and efforts to investors and other stakeholders.[17]

There is no formal disclosure framework that has been specifically developed relating to business reporting on the SDGs; however, reference can and should be made to several useful and evolving guidance documents and related tools[18]:

---

[17] *Integrating the SDGs into Corporate Reporting: A Practical Guide* (Global Reporting Initiative, Principles for Responsible Investment and United Nations Global Compact, 2018), 4.

[18] *Recommendations adapted from In Focus: Addressing Investors Needs in Business Reporting on the SDGs* (Global Reporting Initiative, Principles for Responsible Investment and United Nations Global Compact, 2018), 9.

- The SDG Compass, developed by the UN Global Compact, Global Reporting Initiative (GRI), and the World Business Council for Sustainable Development (WBCSD), includes preliminary information on the SDGs for business.
- The value driver model, developed by the Principles for Responsible Investment (PRI) and the UN Global Compact, uses key business metrics to determine and illustrate how corporate sustainability activities contribute to overall performance and this tool can be used by companies to assess the financial impact of their sustainability strategies and communicate that impact clearly and effectively to investors.
- The 2017 "An Analysis of Goals and Targets," developed by GRI and the UN Global Compact, contains qualitative and quantitative disclosures from globally established reporting frameworks that can be used by business to measure and report on their impact and contribution to the SDG targets.
- "Integrating the SDGs into Corporate Reporting: A Practical Guide," developed by the GRI, PRI, and the UN Global Compact, can be used by companies alongside the Analysis to prioritize the SDGs, set business objectives, improve SDG-related performance, and disclose material information on outputs, outcomes, impacts and contributions to the SDGs.

Part of making the business case for sustainability-related activities is identifying new opportunities that can simultaneously boost the financial performance of companies while supporting the universal drive toward achievement of the SDGs. There are a number of resources available to businesses and other organizations looking for ideas on how to integrate the letter and spirit of the SDGs into their CSR initiatives.[19] For example,

---

[19] An extensive library of information relating to the SDGs, including an inventory that maps existing business tools against the SDGs, is available from SDG Compass (https://sdgcompass-org/business-tools/). SDG Compass suggests that the inventory can be used to explore commonly used business tools that may be useful when assessing an organization's impact on the SDGs. The inventory includes the name and description of the tool, identifies the developer of the tool, and indicates that SDGs to which the tool is applicable.

the UN Global Compact offers participants an extensive toolbox of resources that companies can use to do business responsibly and take action to achieve the SDGs.[20] The "Better Business Better World" report available through the Business & Sustainable Development Commission (http://report.businesscommission.org/) identifies the 60 biggest market opportunities related to the achievement of the SDGs in the areas of food and agriculture (e.g., reducing food waste in the value chain, product reformulation, technology in large-scale farms, micro-irrigation, and urban agriculture); cities (e.g., affordable housing, road safety equipment, water and sanitation infrastructure, office sharing, and car sharing); energy and materials (e.g., expansion of renewables, resource recovery, energy access, shared infrastructure, energy efficiency, and carbon capture and storage); and health and well-being (e.g., weight management programs, better disease management, better maternal and child health, and health care training).

In the executive summary to that report, the Commission offered the following suggestions as to the action that business leaders can and should take in order to "capture their share" of the financial prize available for businesses that effectively commit to contributing to sustainable development[21]:

- Build support for the SDGs as the right growth strategy in their companies and across the business community.
- Incorporate the SDGs into every aspect of company strategy: appointing board members and senior executives to prioritize and drive execution; aiming strategic planning and innovation at sustainable solutions; marketing products and services that inspire consumers to make sustainable choices; and using the SDGs to guide leadership development, women's empowerment at every level, regulatory policy, and capital allocation.
- Drive the transformation to sustainable markets with sector peers and stakeholders including mapping their collective route to a sustainable competitive playing field, identifying

---

[20] https://unglobalcompact.org/sdgs/about

[21] Executive Summary: Better Business Better World (Business & Sustainable Development Commission, January 2017), 8–10.

tipping points, prioritizing the key technology and policy levers, developing the new skill profiles and jobs, quantifying the new financing requirements, and laying out the elements of a just transition.

- Push for a financial system oriented toward longer-term sustainable investment and work to strengthen the flow of capital into sustainable investments by pushing for three things: transparent, consistent league tables of sustainability performance linked to the SDGs; wider and more efficient use of blended finance instruments to share risk and attract much more private finance into sustainable infrastructure; and alignment of regulatory reforms in the financial sector with long-term sustainable investment.

- Rebuild the social contract between business and society by working with governments, consumers, workers, and civil society to achieve the whole range of SDGs, adopting responsible and open policy advocacy and adopting and implementing sustainable business practices for their own activities and those of their supply chain partners (e.g., contributing positively to the communities in which they operate, fair wages and working conditions, training and education, and abolishment of slave and child labor).[22]

---

[22] In a later part of the same report, the Commission stated that: "Treating workers with respect and paying them a decent wage would go a long way to building a more inclusive society and expanding consumer markets. Investing in their training, enabling men and women to fulfill their potential, would deliver further returns through higher labor productivity. And ensuring that the social contract extends from the formal to the informal sector, through full implementation of the UN Guiding Principles on Business and Human Rights, should be non-negotiable." Id. at 17. See also the 10 key recommendations of the Work Group on the connection between the Guiding Principles and the Goals, https://ohchr.org/Documents/Issues/Business/Session18/InfoNoteWGBHR_SDG Recommendations.pdf; Shift's framework for how business enterprises contribute to the SDGs by respecting human rights; and the work being done by the Danish Institute for Human Rights (https://humanrights.dk/business-human-rights)) to provide guidance for businesses on how to use the UN Guiding Principles on Business and Human rights to engage with the SDGs.

CHAPTER 3

Sectoral CSR Commitments

Certain sectors face particular challenges when it comes to corporate social responsibility (CSR) due to the specific nature of the operational activities and the locations of those activities since local governments often are unwilling and/or unable to exercise legal and regulatory responsibility for the environmental and social impacts of the activities. The response to these challenges, often driven by criticisms from a wide range of stakeholders, has been sectoral CSR commitments, which often take the form of a framework of principles with respect to environmental and social issues and emerge from collective CSR initiatives among companies and other stakeholders (e.g., trade unions) involved in particular business sectors and/or with a common interest in a specific social or environmental responsibility issue. Sectoral frameworks usually include targets for compliance with minimum social standards and fundamental environmental protection measures taking into account sector-specific criteria and requirements as decisions are being made.[1] Information on sectoral standards is available from a variety of resources. Certain descriptions of such standards included below are adapted from summaries that prepared and distributed by the Swiss State Secretariat for Economic Affairs (SECO), which oversees various initiatives, and distributes resources, regarding CSR.[2]

An important starting point for identifying and understanding sectoral standards is the Standards Map (sustainabilitymap.org) developed by the International Trade Centre (intracen.org), a joint agency of the

---

[1] *Handbook on Corporate Social Responsibility (CSR) for Employers' Organizations* (European Union CSR for All Project, April 2014), 30.

[2] https://seco.admin.ch/seco/en/home/Aussenwirtschaftspolitik_Wirtschaftliche_Zusammenarbeit/Wirtschaftsbeziehungen/Gesellschaftliche_Verantwortung_der_Unternehmen/CSR_fuer_Branchen.html

World Trade Organization and the UN dedicated to supporting the internationalization of small- and medium-sized enterprises. The Standards Map offers a comprehensive, verified, and transparent information on standards for environmental protection, worker and labor rights, economic development, quality, and food safety, as well as business ethics. As of June 2020, the Standards Map covered more than 250 standards initiatives applicable to more than 80 sectors and 180 countries. The goal of the Standards Map is to help users to engage in sustainable production and trade; review and analyze various standards' requirements and processes; learn about potential certification costs and benefits; access step-by-step guidance on how to comply with requirements; evaluate additional efforts to be in compliance; and monitor progress over time using one self-assessment questionnaires to generate diagnostic reports that provide a detailed analysis of areas for improvement and can be shared online with partners.[3]

Users of the Sustainability Map can begin by identifying which voluntary standards available on the module may be relevant to their business by searching and sorting by sector and/or product; producing region/country and destination region/country. For each standard, the module provides key information on the background of the standard, its requirements, and how it operates. Users can understand the proportion of a standard's requirements that apply to particular sustainability areas such as environment, social, management, quality, and ethics. In addition, users can learn more about their mode of operation; operational scope; potential interoperability; audit and assurance requirements; costs linked to acquiring endorsement; step-by-step guidance as to how to become certified; and technical, financial, or capacity building support provided. The Sustainability Map also allows companies to get a better idea of how

---

[3] www.sustainabilitymap.org. See also the appendices to the ISO 26000 Guidance on Social Responsibility, which include extensive lists of examples of cross-sectoral initiatives as of the date ISO 26000 was completed and tables identifying the ISO 26000 core subjects and practices for integrating social responsibility that have been incorporated into the listed initiatives. *ISO 26000 Guidance on Social Responsibility* (Geneva: International Organization for Standardization, 2010), 87–97.

many environmental, social, economic, ethics, or quality management aspects of their business will need to be changed in order to comply with selected standards.[4]

Another resource is the Multi-Stakeholder Initiative Database (https://msi-database.org/), which was produced as a collaborative effort of The Institute for Multi-Stakeholder Initiative Integrity ("MSI Integrity") and the Duke Human Rights Center at the Kenan Institute for Ethics as an open-access resource for learning about transnational standard-setting MSIs and cataloging publicly available information about the institutional design of MSIs to provide an overview of the governance and operations of these initiatives. The database includes 45 standard-setting MSIs that collectively address a range of human rights, governance, and environmental issues in over 170 countries on six continents, engage over 50 national governments, and regulate over 9,000 companies including more than 65 Fortune Global 500 businesses with combined annual revenues of more than $5.4 trillion.[5]

As discussed elsewhere in this publication, the sponsors of the project prepared a report describing their examination of how the MSIs included in the database were governed and the extent to which they included different stakeholder groups and found that a majority of the standard-setting MSIs failed to meaningfully engage the workers and communities that were most affected by the standards they set. They also found that many MSIs lacked basic institutional elements necessary to effectively set and enforce their own standards.[6] Similar criticisms have been lodged by the UN Working Group for Business and Human Rights, which has reported that there is a belief that MSIs have not met their potential for various reasons including a lack of transparency with respect to accountability mechanisms, which makes it difficult to evaluate their effectiveness, and a relatively weak involvement

---

[4] Id.

[5] https://msi-database.org

[6] The New Regulators? Assessing the Landscape of Multi-Stakeholder Initiatives: Findings from a database of transnational standard-setting multi-stakeholder initiatives (MSI Integrity and the Duke Human Rights Center at the Kenan Institute for Ethics, June 2017).

of governments.[7] On the other hand, it has been argued that industry-specific MSIs that set out to govern corporate behavior have great potential to develop legitimacy.[8]

All Industry

Ethical Trading Initiative

The Ethical Trading Initiative (ETI) (ethicaltrade.org) is a leading alliance of companies, trade unions, and NGOs that promotes respect for workers' rights around the globe and pursues a vision of a world where all workers are free from exploitation and discrimination and enjoy conditions of freedom, security, and equity. Member companies, trade unions, and voluntary organizations work together to tackle the many complex questions about what steps companies should take to trade ethically, and how to make a positive difference to workers' lives. ETI seeks to define best practice in ethical trade and all corporate members of ETI agree to adopt the ETI Base Code of Labour Practice, which is based on International Labour Organisation (ILO) standards. Basic principles included in the ETI Base Code include employment is freely chosen; freedom of association and the right to collective bargaining are respected; working conditions are safe and hygienic; child labor shall not be used; living wages are paid; working hours are not excessive; no discrimination is practiced; regular employment is provided; and no harsh or inhumane treatment is allowed.

Fair Labor Association

The Fair Labor Association (FLA) (fairlabor.org) is an international collaborative effort of universities, civil society organizations, and socially

---

[7] Companion Note II to the Working Group's 2018 Report to the General Assembly: "Corporate human rights due diligence—Getting started, emerging practices, tools and resources" (UN Working Group on Business and Human Rights, October 2018), 17.

[8] Baumann-Pauly, D., J. Nolan, A. van Heerden, and M. Samway. March 7, 2016. "Industry-Specific Multi-Stakeholder Initiatives That Govern Corporate Human Rights Standards: Legitimacy assessments of the Fair Labor Association and the Global Network Initiative." *Journal of Business Ethics*. Published Online.

responsible companies dedicated to protecting workers' rights around the world. FLA places the onus on companies to voluntarily meet internationally recognized labor standards wherever their products are made and offers a collaborative approach allowing civil society organizations, universities, and socially responsible companies to sit at the same table and find effective solutions to labor issues; innovative and sustainable strategies and resources to help companies improve compliance systems; transparent and independent assessments, the results of which are published online; and a mechanism to address the most serious labor rights violations through the third-party complaint process. Companies that affiliate with the FLA are held accountable to implementing the FLA's Code of Conduct across their supply chains and are subject to external assessments by independent external monitors that have satisfied accreditation criteria established by the FLA and described in the FLA's Charter, which also includes a Workplace Code of Conduct and principles of monitoring.

Fairtrade International

Fairtrade International (FI) (fairtrade.net) is a nonprofit multistakeholder association that seeks to change the way trade works through better prices, decent working conditions, and a fairer deal for farmers and workers in developing countries. FI is responsible for setting the Fairtrade Standards and owns the Fairtrade mark. By choosing Fairtrade products, people can create change through their everyday actions, and farming communities can improve their lives and invest in their future. Fairtrade products extend over a broad range of product classifications including cereals, cocoa, coffee, flowers and plants, fresh fruit, gold and precious metals, herbs and spices, herbal teas, honey, nuts, sports balls, sugar, tea, and vegetables, and each product classification has its own standards. Fairtrade also maintains a hazardous materials list. Since Fairtrade's mission is to promote fairer trading conditions for disadvantaged producers, it focuses attention on those countries that fulfill the criteria of Fairtrade's geographical scope policy, which include income per capita, wealth disparity, other economic and social indicators, and Fairtrade's own ability to support producers and achieve long-term impacts.

The Fairtrade Standards (www.fairtrade.net/standards) are the requirements that producers and the businesses who buy their goods have to meet for a product to be Fairtrade certified. The Standards ensure fairer terms of trade between farmers and buyers, protect workers' rights, and provide the framework for producers to build thriving farms and organizations. Economic criteria in the Standards include the Fairtrade Minimum Price, which aims to provide producers with a safety net against falling prices and allow long-term planning, along with a fixed Fairtrade Premium that provides farmers and workers with additional money to invest in improving the quality of their businesses and communities (e.g., by investing in health and education in their communities). Environmental criteria in the Standards emphasize ecologically and agriculturally sound practices, including responsible water and waste management, preserving biodiversity and soil fertility, and minimal use of pesticides and agrochemicals. Fairtrade prohibits the use of several hazardous materials and all genetically modified organisms (GMOs). Social criteria in the Standards for small-scale producers include requirements on democratic self-organization (typically in cooperatives), participatory decision making, transparency, and nondiscrimination (including gender equity). In plantation-type settings where hired labor is the norm, the Standards require companies to operate with nondiscriminatory employment practices, pay rates equal to or higher than the legal or regional minimum wages, freedom of association and collective bargaining rights for the workforce, safeguards for worker safety and health, and facilities to allow workers to manage the Fairtrade Premium. Forced and child labor are prohibited under the Standards.

Extractive/Raw Materials

A useful tool for businesses involved in the extractive sector is the CSR Standards Navigation Tool developed and distributed by the Canadian Government's Office of the Extractive Sector CSR Counselor. While the tool is designed to help Canadian companies, it can be used by businesses everywhere (as well as civil society organizations, communities, and host country governments) to easily access the best practices and guidance outlined in six international standards applicable to the extractive sector. The CSR Standards Navigation Tool's four sections—corporate governance, social, environment, and labor—each feature specific themes.

The themes enable stakeholders to quickly locate relevant international standards, and address particular challenges and risks.[9]

In addition to the standards and initiatives described below, notice should be taken of the following: Alliance for Responsible Mining; Better Biomass; Better Gold Initiative; Diamond Development Initiative; Equitable Origin; Fair Stone; Green-E; Hydropower Sustainability Assessment Protocol; Initiative for Responsible Mining Assurance; and Roundtable on Sustainable Biomaterials. Relevant information is also available from the UN Environment International Resource Panel, which focuses on the economic basis for potential political solutions and measures to separate economic development from the use of resources.

Extractive Industries Transparency Initiative

The Extractive Industries Transparency Initiative (EITI) (www.eiti.org), a nonprofit multistakeholder organization, has developed a widely recognized global standard for promotion of the open and accountable management of oil, gas, and mineral resources that requires the disclosure of information along the extractive industry value chain from the point of extraction, to how revenues make their way through the government, and how they benefit the public. EITI's global standard, which has been implemented in 52 countries with the support of governments, companies, and civil society, is intended to strengthen public and corporate governance, promote understanding of natural resource management, and provide the data to inform reforms for greater transparency and accountability in the extractives sector.

Voluntary Principles on Security and Human Rights

The Voluntary Principles on Security and Human Rights (voluntary principles.org) were established in 2000 as a set of principles designed to guide companies in the extractive sector in maintaining the safety and security of their operations within an operating framework that ensures

---

[9] See *CSR Standards Navigation Tool for the Extractive Sector* (Ottawa: Office of the Extractive Sector CSR Counselor, 2017).

respect for human rights and fundamental freedoms. The Voluntary Principles help mining and oil enterprises evaluate risks and take measures to ensure that they comply with human rights when the safety of these enterprises is protected by security companies, the military, and police forces. The Voluntary Principles are the only human rights guidelines designed specifically for extractive sector companies, and participants in the Voluntary Principles Initiative—including governments, companies, and NGOs—agree to proactively implement or assist in the implementation of the Voluntary Principles. Benefits of joining the Voluntary Principles include operational guidance, risk reduction, and reputational enhancement; and improved collaboration and problem-solving with government and civil society. The Voluntary Principles provide a framework for companies to: conduct an assessment of human rights risks associated with security, including an assessment of whether company actions might heighten or mitigate risk; engage appropriately with public and private security providers; institute human rights screenings for private security forces and encourage the screening of public security forces; take steps to promote the observance of best practices relevant to human rights and security; and develop company systems for reporting and investigating allegations of human rights abuses. Among other things, companies involved with the Voluntary Principles are expected to report annually on activities that support implementation of the Voluntary Principles and formally participate in the governance of the Voluntary Principles.

The Commodity Trading Sector Guidance on Implementing the UN Guiding Principles on Business and Human Rights

The Commodity Trading Sector Guidance on Implementing the UN Guiding Principles on Business and Human Rights was launched in November 2018 for commodity trading companies. Jointly elaborated by companies from the sector, NGOs and the concerned cantonal and federal authorities, this guidance provides companies active in commodity trading with a listing of receipts enabling them implement the UN Guiding Principles for Business and Human Rights as well as the related OECD Guidance described below.

OECD *Due Diligence Guidance*

The OECD has issued due diligence guidance for enterprises operating in the raw materials industry. The OECD Due Diligence Guidance for Responsible Supply Chains of Minerals from Conflict-Affected and High-Risk Areas helps enterprises operating in the raw materials industry in conflict-affected and high-risk areas to exercise their due diligence for the supply chain and thus prevent them from indirectly supporting conflicts or contributing to human rights abuses. The guidance provides detailed recommendations to help companies respect human rights and avoid contributing to conflict through their mineral purchasing decisions and practices. The core guidance document and two mineral-specific supplements explain how multinational companies sourcing gold, tin, tantalum, and tungsten can avoid fueling conflict and responsibly source and trade minerals. The OECD Due Diligence Guidance for Meaningful Stakeholder Engagement in the Extractive Sector helps mining, oil and gas enterprises take stakeholder interests into account (e.g. local communities, employees, artisanal miners) within the framework of their corporate due diligence.

Agriculture, Forestry, and Fishing

Several important environmental and social concerns must be addressed simultaneously when considering the use and ownership of agricultural lands. For example, land-use systems should be transparent and fair in order to promote access to land and other natural resources, particularly in poorer communities and in rural areas of developing countries. In addition, the need to secure food supply around the world means that steps must be taken to ensure and facilitate responsible investment in agriculture and food systems. Given the value chains for agricultural products often extend across border and oceans, enterprises must exercise due diligence to identify and eliminate environmentally and socially irresponsible actions by producers.

In addition to the standards and initiative described below, notice should be taken of the following: Alliance for Water Stewardship; Better Cotton Initiative; Bonsucro; Equitable Food Initiative; Fair Flowers

Fair Plants; Florverde Sustainable Flowers; Food Alliance; Global Coffee Platform; International Seafood Sustainability Foundation; Marine Aquarium Council; Roundtable on Responsible Soy; and Wildlife Friendly Enterprise Network. The Voluntary Guidelines on the Responsible Governance of Tenure of the United Nations advise countries and enterprises, among others, on internationally recognized practices for land-use systems, helping to improve the relevant country's regulations and the corresponding policies, increasing transparency on these matters and honing the skills of the competent authorities. The Principles for Responsible Investment in Agriculture and Food Systems identify the most important stakeholders and their responsibility as regards sustainable investment in agriculture and food systems, and serve as a framework for their activities. The OECD-FAO Guidance for Responsible Agricultural Supply Chains helps agricultural enterprises exercise their due diligence for a sustainable value chain based on international standards.

Forest Stewardship Council

The Forest Stewardship Council (FSC) (fsc.org) is a multistakeholder initiative focused on the promotion of environmentally sound, socially beneficial, and economically prosperous management of the world's forests and currently operates in more than 80 countries, wherever forests are present. FSC certification ensures that products come from responsibly managed forests that provide environmental, social, and economic benefits. The FSC claims to be the world's strongest certification system, in terms of global reach, robustness of certification criteria and number of businesses involved in the system. The FSC has developed regionally appropriate guidelines and standards for sustainable forest management and FSC certification is frequently required as a condition to contracting with governmental agencies. To achieve its mission and vision, FSC has developed a set of 10 principles and 57 Criteria that apply to FSC-certified forests around the world. The FSC's principles include the following:

- *Principle 1: Compliance with laws and FSC principles*: Forest management shall respect all applicable laws of the country in which they occur, and international treaties and agreements to which the country is a signatory, and comply with all FSC Principles and Criteria.

- *Principle 2: Tenure and use rights and responsibilities*: Long-term tenure and use rights to the land and forest resources shall be clearly defined, documented, and legally established.
- *Principle 3: Indigenous peoples' rights*: The legal and customary rights of indigenous peoples to own, use, and manage their lands, territories, and resources shall be recognized and respected.
- *Principle 4: Community relations and worker's rights*: Forest management operations shall maintain or enhance the long-term social and economic well-being of forest workers and local communities.
- *Principle 5: Benefits from the forest*: Forest management operations shall encourage the efficient use of the forest's multiple products and services to ensure economic viability and a wide range of environmental and social benefits.
- *Principle 6: Environmental impact*: Forest management shall conserve biological diversity and its associated values, water resources, soils, and unique and fragile ecosystems and landscapes, and, by so doing, maintain the ecological functions and the integrity of the forest.
- *Principle 7: Management plan*: A management plan—appropriate to the scale and intensity of the operations—shall be written, implemented, and kept up to date. The long-term objectives of management, and the means of achieving them, shall be clearly stated.
- *Principle 8: Monitoring and assessment*: Monitoring shall be conducted appropriate to the scale and intensity of forest management to assess the condition of the forest, yields of forest products, chain of custody, management activities, and their social and environmental impacts.
- *Principle 9: Maintenance of high conservation value forests*: Management activities in high conservation value forests shall maintain or enhance the attributes that define such forests. Decisions regarding high conservation value forests shall always be considered in the context of a precautionary approach.

- *Principle 10: Plantations*: Plantations shall be planned and managed in accordance with Principles and Criteria 1 to 9 and Principle 10 and its Criteria. While plantations can provide an array of social and economic benefits, and can contribute to satisfying the world's needs for forest products, they should complement the management of, reduce pressures on, and promote the restoration and conservation of natural forests.

International Sustainability and Carbon Certification

International Sustainability and Carbon Certification (ISCC) (iscc-system.org) is a globally leading certification system that offers solutions to address sustainability requirements for all feedstocks and markets. ISCC aims at the implementation of highest sustainability requirements; ecological sustainability; protection of land with high biodiversity value or high carbon stock; deforestation free supply chains; environmentally responsible production to protect soil, water, and air; social sustainability; safe working conditions; compliance with human, labor, and land rights; and compliance with laws and international treaties. ISCC was developed through an open multistakeholder process that included 250+ international associations, corporations, research institutions, and NGOs from around the world. ISCC association currently has 100+ members and ISCC engages in continuous stakeholder dialogue and supports regional and technical stakeholder committees in Europe, Asia/Pacific, North America, and South America. Independent third-party certification against ISCC standards can be applied in various markets including the bioenergy sector, the food and feed market and the chemical market to demonstrate compliance with high ecological and social sustainability requirements, greenhouse gas emissions savings, and traceability throughout the supply chain.

Marine Stewardship Council

The Marine Stewardship Council (MSC) (msc.org) is an international nonprofit organization established to protect oceans and address the problem of unsustainable fishing and safeguard seafood supplies for the future. MSC uses its eco-label and fishery certification program to contribute to the health of the world's oceans by recognizing and rewarding sustainable fishing practices, influencing the choices people make when buying seafood and working with its partners to transform the seafood market to a sustainable basis. The MSC Standards, which include the Fisheries Standard and the Chain of Custody Standard for traceability, meet international best practice guidelines for certification and eco-labeling and were developed through consultation with the fishing industry, scientists, seafood producers and brands, conservationists, experts, and stakeholders in order to set credible standards for sustainable fishing and supply chain traceability. Organizations meet these standards in order to demonstrate the sustainability of their products and the blue MSC label makes it easy for everyone to choose seafood which has been caught by fisheries which care for the environment.

Program for Endorsement of Forest Certification

The Program for Endorsement of Forest Certification (PEFC) (pefc.org) is an international nonprofit NGO that has become a leading global alliance of national forest certification systems dedicated to promoting sustainable forest management through independent third-party certification. PEFC is a membership organization that claims to be the largest forest certification system in the world and is based in Geneva with more than 70 members located around the world including national certification systems, NGOs, labor unions, business, trade associations, forest owner organizations, and committed individuals. PEFC's 51 national members are independent, national organizations that develop and implement the PEFC system within their country. PEFC endorses national forest certification systems developed through multistakeholder processes and tailored to local priorities and conditions, thus providing forest owners, from the large to the small, with a tool to demonstrate their responsible practices, while empowering consumers and companies to buy sustainably.

Roundtable on Sustainable Palm Oil

The Roundtable on Sustainable Palm Oil (RSPO) (rspo.org) is a not-for-profit that unites stakeholders from the seven sectors of the palm oil industry (i.e., oil palm producers, processors or traders, consumer goods manufacturers, retailers, banks/investors, and environmental and social NGOs) to develop and implement global standards for sustainable palm oil. The RSPO is a multistakeholder learning and criteria development process formed to advance the production, procurement, finance, and use of sustainable palm oil products; develop, implement, verify, assure, and periodically review credible global standards for the entire supply chain of sustainable palm oil; monitor and evaluate the economic, environmental, and social impacts of the uptake of sustainable palm oil in the market; and engage and commit all stakeholders throughout the supply chain, including governments and consumers. The RSPO has developed a set of environmental and social criteria that companies must comply with in order to produce Certified Sustainable Palm Oil. When they are properly applied, these criteria can help to minimize the negative impact of palm oil cultivation on the environment and communities in palm oil-producing regions. The RSPO has more than 4,000 members worldwide who represent all links along the palm oil supply chain. They have committed to produce, source, and/or use sustainable palm oil certified by the RSPO.

Sustainable Forestry Initiative

The Sustainable Forestry Initiative (SFI) (sfiprogram.org) is a solutions-oriented sustainability organization that collaborates on forest-based conservation and community initiatives that demonstrate and enhance our shared quality of life while providing supply chain assurances through standards, data, and authentic stories. SFI works with the forest sector, brand owners, conservation groups, resource professionals, landowners, educators, local communities, Indigenous peoples, governments, and universities. SFI standards and on product labels help consumers make responsible purchasing decisions. More than 360 million acres/147 million hectares of forestland is certified to the SFI Forest Management Standard. These lands stretch from Canada's boreal forest to the U.S. South. Additionally, SFI oversees the SFI Forest Partners® Program, which aims to increase supply of certified forest products, the SFI Conservation and Community Partnerships Grant Program, which funds research and community building, and Project Learning Tree®, which educates teachers and youth about forests and the environment.

Finance

The explosive and continuing growth in the types of investment instruments and the complexity of business models in the financial sector has created a number of risks for potential adverse effects on the environment and society. As noted elsewhere in this publication, the International Finance Corporation (IFC) has adopted a set of Performance Standards to guide its investments and these standards have been incorporated by private banks and other financial institutions into their assessment of project finance and project-related corporate loan proposals through their commitment to adhere to the Equator Principles (EPs) (equator-principles.com). The EPs is a risk management framework adopted by financial institutions for determining, assessing, and managing environmental and social risk in projects and is primarily intended to provide a minimum standard for due diligence and monitoring to support responsible risk decision making. The EPs apply globally, to all industry sectors and to four financial products: project finance advisory services, project finance, project-related corporate loans, and bridge loans. As of 2019, the EPs had been officially adopted by almost 100 Equator Principles Financing Institutions (EPFIs) in 37 countries covering the majority of international project finance debt within developed and emerging markets. EPFIs commit to implementing the EPs in their internal environmental and social policies, procedures, and standards for financing projects and will not provide project finance or project-related corporate loans to projects where the client will not, or is unable to, comply with the EPs. The EPs have greatly increased the attention and focus on social/community standards and responsibility, including robust standards for indigenous peoples, labor standards, and consultation with locally affected communities within the project finance market and have contributed to the promotion of convergence around common environmental and social standards (e.g., multilateral development banks, such as the European Bank for Reconstruction and Development, and export credit agencies are increasingly drawing on the same standards as the EPs.

OECD Responsible Business Conduct in the Financial Sector is intended to provide the financial sector (including institutional investors) with tools for implementing the OECD Guidelines for Multinational

Enterprises. In 2019, the European Parliament overwhelmingly approved an EU Regulation for Sustainability-related Disclosures in the Financial Services Sector that called on financial institutions to disclose sustainability risks and impacts. The Regulation introduces transparency rules for financial institutions on the integration of sustainability risks and impacts in their processes and financial products, including reporting on adherence to internationally recognized standards for due diligence. It also notes that when reporting on due diligence, practitioners "should consider the due diligence guidance for responsible business conduct developed by the Organisation for Economic Cooperation and Development."

The UNEP Inquiry: Design of a Sustainable Financial System has been established to collect best practice examples and experience from different countries and define strategies for finance systems to take a better approach to sustainable development requirements. Further initiatives in the finance sector can be expected. For example, in late 2018, UN Secretary-General António Guterres asked Michael R. Bloomberg, the UN Special Envoy for Climate Action, to lead a private-sector initiative to support a global mobilization of private finance in response to the challenge of climate change. Senior executives of seven major private-sector institutions from across the investment chain—Allianz Global Investors, AXA, Enel, Goldman Sachs, HSBC, Japan's Government Pension Investment Fund (GPIF), and Macquarie—agreed to join Bloomberg as chair in creating the Climate Finance Leadership Initiative to mobilize and scale private capital for climate solutions.

Security

SECO noted that countries and enterprises often commission private military and security companies to protect their safety in armed conflicts and areas where the rule of law is under threat and referred to the Montreux Document as an overview of the international legal obligations of private military and security companies deployed in armed conflicts and a source of advice on methods that countries can use to meet their international legal obligations. At the enterprise level, signatories to the International Code of Conduct for Private Security Service Providers undertake to adhere to human rights and international humanitarian law in areas where the rule of law is under threat. SECO recommended the toolkit "Addressing Security and Human Rights Challenges in Complex Environments" for good practices when working with public security forces and private security providers.

Garment and Footwear

SECO pointed out that the garment and footwear sector is one of the biggest consumer goods sectors in the world and poses potential risks relating to adverse effects on society and the environment arising from the direct operations of an enterprise or its value chain.

Finnish Textile & Fashion

Finnish Textile & Fashion (FTF), the central organization for textile, clothing, and fashion companies in Finland, suggested that responsible companies typically share the following attributes[10]:

- They strive to do more than required by law.
- They take into account the needs and expectations of their stakeholders and engage in dialogue with them.
- They strive to have a positive impact on stakeholders other than their shareholders.
- They work with partners to develop corporate responsibility throughout the supply chain.
- They strive to minimize the negative financial, social, and ecological effects of their operations.
- They ensure that their partners are aware of their codes of conduct.
- They openly and transparently report and communicate on the positive and negative effects of their operations.

---

[10] *Finnish Textile & Fashion Corporate Responsibility Manual* (Helsinki: Finnish Textile & Fashion, 2016), 16.

Essential characteristics of a responsible company identified by FTF included[11]:

- Corporate responsibility is included in the company's basic philosophy—it is present in the values, vision, and strategy.
- The company has clear operating principles, models, and instructions to guide corporate responsibility.
- The senior management is committed to the matter and has made sure that the personnel are also committed.
- Measurement focuses on the most important questions.
- The outcomes of corporate responsibility are measured reliably and reported on openly and transparently using widely-accepted reporting frameworks such as the Global Reporting Initiative.
- Development is goal-oriented.
- The operates in solid interaction with its key stakeholders.

FTF recommended that companies follow a simple multistep process to get started with CSR[12]:

- Reviewing and describing the current status of the company's programs and actions with respect to corporate responsibility
- Defining the corporate responsibility themes that are material to company's success
- Defining the target level for corporate responsibility with respect to each of the company's material corporate responsibility themes
- Formalizing the target levels into corporate responsibility commitments
- Establishing corporate responsibility principles and policies (e.g., code of conduct and detailed guidelines and principles on specific topics such as the environment, human resources, and procurement)

---

[11] Id.

[12] Id. at 10.

- Target corporate responsibility program which lays out a three- to five-year program of actions to be taken on the material corporate responsibility themes with specific objectives and indicators and allocations of authority and accountability
- Measurement and monitoring of performance against the selected objectives and indicators and adjustment of strategies and objectives based on regularly reviews of performance (no less frequently than annually)
- Verified reporting on the results of the corporate responsibility program and communication of the results to stakeholders using multiple channels

OECD Due Diligence Guidance for Responsible Supply Chains in the Garment and Footwear Sector

The leading source of guidance in this sector is the OECD Due Diligence Guidance for Responsible Supply Chains in the Garment and Footwear Sector, which supports the implementation of the OECD Guidelines for Multinational Enterprises and due diligence procedures relating to human rights and the environment in the value chain.

Worldwide Responsible Accredited Production (Wrap)

Worldwide Responsible Accredited Production ("WRAP") (wrap compliance.org) is an independent, objective, nonprofit team of global social compliance experts dedicated to promoting safe, lawful, humane, and ethical manufacturing around the world through certification and education. WRAP was formed out of the desire to create an independent and objective body to help apparel and footwear factories around the world verify that they are operating in compliance with local laws and internationally accepted standards of ethical workplace practices. Today, WRAP has grown to become a global leader in social compliance and a trusted independent supply chain partner for dozens of companies around the world. Its comprehensive facility-based model has made it the world's largest independent social compliance certification program for the apparel/textile industry and there are more than 2,200 WRAP-certified facilities found throughout the world employing over two million workers.

The WRAP Principles are based on generally accepted international workplace standards, local laws, and workplace regulations, and include the spirit or language of relevant conventions of the International Labor Organization. The Principles encompass human resources management, health and safety, environmental practices, and legal compliance including import/export and customs compliance and security standards. The WRAP Certification Program's objective is to independently monitor and certify compliance with these standards, to ensure that sewn products are being produced under lawful, humane, and ethical conditions. Participating facilities voluntarily commit to ensuring that their manufacturing practices will meet these standards, and further commit to passing along, on their part, the expectation that their contractors and suppliers likewise comply with these standards.

Technology and Telecommunications

The Global Network Initiative (GNI) (globalnetworkinitiative.org) is a multistakeholder platform developed from consultations among companies, human rights and press freedom organizations, academics, and investors to provide guidance to technology companies on how best to respect the rights of their users in the face of requests from governments to censor content, restrict access to communications services, or hand over user data. GNI participants work together in two mutually supporting ways. The GNI Principles ("the Principles") and Implementation Guidelines provide an evolving framework for responsible company decision making in support of freedom of expression and privacy rights. As participation in the GNI expands, the Principles are taking root as global standard for human rights in the information, communication, and technology (ICT) sector. The GNI also collectively advocates with governments and international institutions for laws and policies that promote and protect freedom of expression and privacy.

CHAPTER 4

CSR-Related Reporting and Management Standards

It is now widely acknowledged that best practices relating to the implementation of effective corporate social responsibility (CSR) practices must include a commitment to transparency and reporting on CSR-related activities and impacts to the organization's stakeholders, either as part of or in addition to any other disclosures that may be required of the organization by law or statute. In addition, CSR is like any other important strategic initiative and should be carried out pursuant to a formal sustainability management system and process that includes due diligence, development, and implementation of strategic and operational goals and plans, monitoring, and assessment of impacts overseen by the members of the governing body of the organization. Several of the most influential and widely used CSR-related standards have specifically addressed reporting and management and are briefly described below in this chapter.[1]

Reporting Standards

In order to know whether or not the CSR initiative and its related commitments are actually improving the company's performance it is necessary to have in place procedures for reporting and verification, each of which are important tools for measuring change and communicating those changes to the company's stakeholders. Hohnen and Potts described reporting as "communicating with stakeholders about a firm's

---

[1] For further discussion, see Gutterman, A. 2020. *Sustainability Reporting and Communications*. New York, NY: Business Expert Press, and Gutterman, A. 2020. *Sustainability Management*. New York, NY: Routledge.

economic, environmental and social management and performance" and verification, which is often referred to as "assurance," as a form of measurement that involves on-site inspections and review of management systems to determine levels of conformity to particular criteria set out in codes and standards to which the company may have agreed to adhere.[2] Verification procedures should be tailored to the company's organizational culture and the specific elements of the company's CSR strategy and commitments; however, it is common for companies to rely on internal audits, industry (i.e., peer) and stakeholder reviews and professional third-party audits. Verification procedures should be established before a specific CSR initiative is undertaken and should be included in the business case for the initiative.[3]

When establishing plans for reporting and verification it is useful to obtain and review copies of reports that have been done and published by comparable companies. Reports of larger companies are generally available on their corporate websites and extensive archives of past CSR-focused reports can be accessed through various online platforms such as CorporateRegister.com, a widely recognized global online directory of corporate responsibility reports. It is also important to have a good working understanding of well-known reporting and verification initiatives such as the Global Reporting Initiative Standards; the AccountAbility AA1000 series; the United Nations Global Compact; and the International Auditing and Assurance Standards Board ISAE 3000 standard. Country-specific information is also available through professional organizations such as the Canadian Chartered Professional Accountants, which has published an extensive report on sustainability reporting in Canada.

---

[2] Hohnen, P., (Author) and J. Potts, ed. 2007. *Corporate Social Responsibility: An Implementation Guide for Business*, 67. Winnipeg, Canada: International Institute for Sustainable Development.

[3] Companies using the Future-Fit business goals recommended by the Future-Fit Business Network can adopt the "fitness criteria" associated with each of the goals. See the discussion of the Future-Fit business goals in *Future-Fit Business Framework, Part 1: Concepts, Principles and Goals* (Future-Fit Foundation, Release 1, May 2016), 25, FutureFitBusiness.org.

Global Reporting Initiative

The Global Reporting Initiative (GRI) (www.globalreporting.org) was founded in 1997 by the Coalition for Environmentally Responsible Economics (CERES) in Boston, Massachusetts, to develop a standardized sustainability reporting framework that would effectively capture and describe the sustainability activities that transpire in the economic, environmental, and social aspects of organizational operations.[4] The goal of the GRI has been to serve as a multistakeholder developed international independent organization that helps businesses, governments, and other organizations understand and communicate the impact of business on critical sustainability issues such as climate change, human rights, corruption, and many others. In so doing, reporting enterprises can make better decisions regarding the actions that should be taken toward a more sustainable economy and world. When it was formed, the GRI was one of the pioneers of sustainability reporting. Since then, the GRI has been a primary driver of transforming sustainability reporting from a niche practice to one now adopted by a growing majority of organizations. The GRI's standards are the world's most widely used with respect to sustainability reporting and disclosure and are available for use by public agencies, firms, and other organizations wishing to understand and communicate aspects of their economic, environmental, and social performance. The GRI's reporting standards are based on widely recognized international norms and normative frameworks on sustainability such as the UN Guiding Principles on Business and Human Rights, the ILO Conventions, the ten principles of the UN Global Compact, and the OECD Guidelines for Multinational Enterprises.[5]

The latest version of the GRI's sustainability reporting framework was published, following extensive consultation, in October 2016 and formally went into effect for reports and other materials published on or

---

[4] Adapted from a description of the evolution of the Global Reporting Initiative included in Mink, K. 2012. *The Effects of Organizational Structure on Sustainability Report Compliance*, 12–13. Purdue University College of Technology Masters' Thesis, Available at http://docs.lib.purdue.edu/techmasters/62

[5] For detailed discussion of the GRI Standards, see Gutterman, A. 2020. *Sustainability Reporting and Communications*. New York, NY: Business Expert Press.

after July 1, 2018. Reporting is required in three categories: economic (e.g., economic performance, indirect economic impacts, procurement practices etc.); environmental (e.g., materials, energy, water, transport, environmental grievance mechanisms etc.); and social, which includes labor practices and decent work (e.g., employment, occupational health and safety, training and education etc.), human rights (e.g., nondiscrimination, forced or compulsory labor, indigenous rights etc.), society (e.g., local communities etc.), and product responsibility (e.g., customer health and safety, product and service labeling, customer privacy etc.). As has been the case with previous version of the GRI framework, companies are expected to follow four fundamental principles when defining the content of their sustainability reports: materiality (i.e., the report should cover topics that reflect the company's significant economic, environmental, and social impacts), stakeholder inclusiveness (i.e., the report should identify the company's stakeholders and explain how the company has responded to their reasonable expectations and interests), sustainability context (i.e., performance should be explained in the wider context of sustainability), and completeness (i.e., the report should cover material topics and their boundaries, sufficient to reflect significant economic, environmental, and social impacts, and to enable stakeholders to assess organizational performance). Quality standards applicable to sustainability reported based on the GRI framework include accuracy, balance, clarity, comparability, reliability, and timeliness.

International Integrated Reporting Framework

The International Integrated Reporting Council, (IIRC; www.theiirc.org) is a global coalition of regulators, investors, companies, standard setters, the accounting profession, and NGOs dedicated to promoting communications about value creation as the next step in the evolution of corporate reporting.[6] The IIRC, which was founded in August 2010, released

---

[6] Carrots & Sticks: Global Trends in Sustainability Reporting Regulation and Policy (KPMG International, the Global Research Initiative (GRI), the United Nations Environment Programme (UNEP), and the Centre for Corporate Governance in Africa, 2016), available at www.carrotsandsticks.net, 25.

its International Integrated Reporting Framework in December 2013 as a guide that companies could use to describe how their governance structure creates value in the short, medium, and long term; supports decision making that takes into account risks and includes mechanisms for addressing ethical issues; exceeds legal requirements; and ensures that the culture, ethics, and values of the company are reflected in its use of and effects on the company's "capitals" (described to include financial, manufactured, intellectual, human, social and relationship, and natural (i.e., the environment and natural resources) forms of value) and stakeholder relationships.[7]

The IRRC Framework was aimed primarily at producing information for long-term investors and providing companies with guiding principles and content elements that would govern the content of their integrated reports.[8] The executive summary to the Framework explained that the drafters had taken a principles-based approach with the intent to strike an appropriate balance between flexibility and prescription that recognized the wide variation in individual circumstances of different organizations while enabling a sufficient degree of comparability across organizations to meet relevant information needs. According to the executive summary, the following guiding principles underpin the preparation of an integrated report, informing the content of the report and how information is presented[9]:

- *Strategic focus and future orientation*: An integrated report should provide insight into the organization's strategy, and how it relates to the organization's ability to create value in the short, medium, and long term, and to its use of and effects on the capitals
- *Connectivity of information*: An integrated report should show a holistic picture of the combination, interrelatedness, and

---

[7] DeSimone, P. 2014. *Board Oversight of Sustainability Issues: A Study of the S&P 500.* IRRC Institute, 7.

[8] *The International <IR> Framework* (International Integrated Reporting Council, December 2013).

[9] Id. at 5.

dependencies between the factors that affect the organization's ability to create value over time

- *Stakeholder relationships*: An integrated report should provide insight into the nature and quality of the organization's relationships with its key stakeholders, including how and to what extent the organization understands, takes into account and responds to their legitimate needs and interests
- *Materiality*: An integrated report should disclose information about matters that substantively affect the organization's ability to create value over the short, medium, and long term
- *Conciseness*: An integrated report should be concise
- *Reliability and completeness*: An integrated report should include all material matters, both positive and negative, in a balanced way and without material error
- *Consistency and comparability*: The information in an integrated report should be presented: (a) on a basis that is consistent over time and (b) in a way that enables comparison with other organizations to the extent it is material to the organization's own ability to create value over time.

In addition, the executive summary to the Framework explained that reports should include the following content elements, each of which are fundamentally linked to each other and are not mutually exclusive[10]:

- *Organizational overview and external environment*: What does the organization do and what are the circumstances under which it operates?
- *Governance*: How does the organization's governance structure support its ability to create value in the short, medium, and long term?
- *Business model*: What is the organization's business model?
- *Risks and opportunities*: What are the specific risks and opportunities that affect the organization's ability to create

---

[10] Id.

value over the short, medium, and long term, and how is the organization dealing with them?

- *Strategy and resource allocation*: Where does the organization want to go and how does it intend to get there?
- *Performance*: To what extent has the organization achieved its strategic objectives for the period and what are its outcomes in terms of effects on the capitals?
- *Outlook*: What challenges and uncertainties is the organization likely to encounter in pursuing its strategy, and what are the potential implications for its business model and future performance?
- *Basis of presentation*: How does the organization determine what matters to include in the integrated report and how are such matters quantified or evaluated?

International Standards of Accounting and Reporting

The Intergovernmental Working Group of Experts on International Standards of Accounting and Reporting (ISAR), which is hosted by the United Nations Conference on Trade and Development (UNCTAD), has issued a series of reports relating to nonfinancing reporting that provide guidance to companies on environmental accounting and reporting, corporate governance disclosure, and corporate responsibility reporting in annual reports. ISAR assists developing countries and economies in transition in the implementation of best practices for accounting and corporate governance with the goal of enhancing the investment climate in those countries and economies and promoting sustainable development.

Sustainability Accounting Standards Board

The Sustainability Accounting Standards Board (SASB) (www.sasb.org) is a U.S.-based independent standards-setting organization for sustainability accounting standards that was incorporated in July 2011 to meet the needs of investors by fostering high-quality disclosure of material sustainability information. The SASB has established industry-based sustainability standards for the recognition and disclosure of material environmental, social, and governance impacts by companies traded on U.S. exchanges.[11] The standards focus on known trends and uncertainties that are reasonably likely to affect the financial condition or operating performance of a company and therefore would be considered material under mandatory disclosure requirements, such as Regulation S-K applicable to disclosures made by U.S. reporting companies in the public filings with the Securities and Exchange Commission (SEC). The SASB is an ANSI-accredited standards developer; however, it is not affiliated with FASB, GASB, IASB, or any other accounting standards board.

SASB standards do not include a scoring system, instead the focus is on providing companies with a standardized methodology that can be deployed when reporting sustainability performance through their regular regulatory reporting to the SEC on Forms 10-K and 10-Q (i.e., an "integrated reporting" approach as opposed to separate nonfinancial reports). SASB's standards enable comparison of peer performance and benchmarking within an industry and the SASB has gathered the support of Bloomberg LP and the Rockefeller Foundation. The SASB publishes the SASB Implementation Guide for Companies that provides the structure and the key considerations for companies seeking to implement sustainability accounting standards within their existing business functions and processes.[12] The Guide helps companies to select sustainability topics; assess the current state of disclosure and management; embed SASB standards into financial reporting and management processes; support disclosure and management with internal control; and present information for disclosure. The SASB's online resource library also includes annual reports on the state of disclosure, industry briefs and standards, and guidance on stakeholder engagement. Companies should monitor CSR disclosures by their peers and the SASB library has examples of disclosures made by companies in annual reports filed with the SEC on Form 10-K.

[11] Carrots & Sticks: Global Trends in Sustainability Reporting Regulation and Policy (KPMG International, the Global Research Initiative (GRI), the United Nations Environment Programme (UNEP), and the Centre for Corporate Governance in Africa, 2016), available at www.carrotsandsticks.net, 25.
[12] For a detailed discussion of the activities of the SASB, see Gutterman, A. 2020. *Sustainability Reporting and Communications*. New York, NY: Business Expert Press.

Management Standards

A management system refers to what an organization does to manage its structures, processes, activities, and resources in order that its products or services meet the organization's objectives, such as satisfying the customer's quality requirements, complying with regulations, and/or meeting environmental objectives. Elements of a management system include policy, planning, implementation and operations, performance assessment, improvement, and management review. By systemizing the way it does things, an organization can increase efficiency and effectiveness, make sure that nothing important is left out of the process and ensure that everyone is clear about who is responsible for doing what, when, how, why, and where. While all organizations should benefit from some form of management system, they are particularly important for larger organizations or ones with complicated processes. Management systems have been used for a number of years in sectors such as aerospace, automobiles, defense, and health care.

Organizations implement management systems for a variety of reasons such as achieving business objectives, increasing understanding of current operations and the likely impact of change, communicating knowledge, demonstrating compliance with legal requirements and/or industry standards, establishing "best practice," ensuring consistency, setting priorities, or changing behavior. Organizations often have more than one management system to deal with different activities or assets and integrate several related operational areas. For example, a customer relationship management system (CRM) might be launched to manage relationships with customers. A preventive maintenance management (PMM) and financial management systems may be used to preserve the value of organizational assets and human resource management systems merge and integrate the principles of human resource management with information technology. Other management systems focus on managing all relevant areas of operation in relation to a specific aspect such as quality, environment, health and safety, information technology, data security, corporate social responsibility, risk management, and business continuity.

Even though they may not realize it, all organizations have some sort of management system—"the way things get done"—in place. Elements of the system may be documented in the form of policies and checklists, but much of the system is based on unwritten rules and customs. The interest of organizational leaders in management systems is based not only on the desire to understand how things are currently done but also to find out how "things should be done" in order to improve organizational performance. Fortunately, reference can be made to management system standards, such as those promulgated by the International Organization for Standardization (ISO) (www.iso.org), which are intended to provide all organizations with easy access to international "state-of-the-art" models that they can follow in implementing their own management systems. Management systems standards are concerned with processes, meaning the way that organizations go about carrying out their required work—they are not product and service standards, although processes certainly impact the quality of the organization's final products and services.

Many of the ISO standards are intended to be generic, which means that they can be applied to any organization, large or small, whatever its product or service; in any sector of activity; and whether it is a business enterprise, a public administration, or a government department. The standards specify the requirements for a management system (e.g., objectives, policy, planning, implementation and operation, performance assessment, improvement, and management review); however, the actual format of the system must be determined by the organization itself taking into account its specific goals and the environment in which it operates. ISO standards are available for management systems covering a broad range of topics including quality (ISO 9001, discussed below), environment (ISO 14001, discussed below), medical device quality (ISO 13485), medical devise risk (ISO 14971), information security (ISO 27001 and ISO 27002), business continuity (ISO 22301), supply chain security (ISO 28000), corporate risk (ISO 31000), food safety (ISO 22000), and management auditing (ISO 19011).

Organizations interested in improving their practices with respect to social responsibility, including engagement with their stakeholders, may refer to ISO 26000; however, ISO 26000 is not a management system standard and does not contain requirements. Instead, ISO 26000 explains the core subjects and associated issues relating to social responsibility including organizational governance, human rights, labor practices, the environment, fair operating practices, consumer issues, and community involvement and development. For each core subject, information is provided on its scope, including key issues; its relationship to social responsibility; related principles and considerations; and related actions and expectations. For example, with respect to labor practices, one of the core subjects, organizations are reminded to integrate consideration of the following issues into their policies, organizational culture, strategies, and operations: employment and employment relationships; conditions of work and social protection; social dialogue; health and safety at work; and human development and training in the workplace.[13]

Organizations may, and often do, seek and obtain certification by independent outside parties that their management systems conform to the requirements of ISO standards. In lieu of certification, or in preparation for a certification audit, organizations should conduct formal self-assessments on a regular basis that cover quality management system requirements; management responsibility requirements; resource management requirements; product realization requirements (e.g., planning, determination of customer requirements, design, and development, purchasing, production and service provision); and measurement, analysis, and improvement requirements.[14]

AccountAbility

AccountAbility (http://accountability.org/) is a global consulting and standards firm formed in 1995 that works with business, governments, and multilateral organizations to advance responsible business practices and improve their long-term performance. AccountAbility works with organizations to improve their performance through their sustainability strategy, the environmental and social impact of their operations, innovation and growth opportunities, stakeholder engagement, and the

---

[13] See International Organization for Standardization, ISO 26000 Guidance on Social Responsibility: Discovering ISO 26000 (2014) and *Handbook for Implementers of ISO 26000, Global Guidance Standard on Social Responsibility by Small and Medium Sized Businesses* (Middlebury VT: ECOLOGIA, 2011).

[14] See http://cw.routledge.com/textbooks/eresources/9781856176842/Requirement_checklist.pdf

reporting of their information. AccountAbility provides advisory services in areas such as strategy and governance, materiality review, stakeholder engagement, impact assessment, and reporting and communications and performs and publishes research relating to collaborative governance, impact, materiality, responsible competitiveness, stakeholder engagement, and sustainability leadership. AccountAbility also offers training in the field of sustainability assurance and licenses its methodologies to sustainability professionals worldwide for their use in conducting sustainability-related assurance engagements.

AccountAbility has become widely recognized for its AA1000 Series of Standards, which are principles-based standards and frameworks that have been adopted and used by a broad spectrum of organizations—global businesses, private enterprises, governments, and civil societies—to demonstrate leadership and performance in accountability, responsibility and sustainability and guide their approach to sustainability strategy, governance, and operational management. The AA1000 Series includes the AA1000 AccountAbility Principles Standard (AA1000AP, 2018) (a framework for an organization to identify, prioritize, and respond to its sustainability challenges); the AA 1000 Assurance Standard (AA1000AS, 2008 with 2018 Addendum) (a methodology for assurance practitioners to evaluate the nature and extent to which an organization adheres to the AccountAbility Principles)[15]; and the AA1000 Stakeholder Engagement Standard (AA1000SES, 2015) (a framework to help organizations ensure stakeholder engagement processes are purpose-driven, robust, and deliver results)[16]. Each of the AccoutAbility standards was developed through a multistakeholder consultation process to help organizations become more

---

[15] The AA1000 AccountAbility Assurance Standard (2008) provides a methodology for use by sustainability professionals for sustainability-related assurance engagements to evaluate the nature and extent to which an organization adheres to the AccountAbility Principles. Separate Guidance notes for assurance providers, reporting organizations, and stakeholders on AA1000AS (2008) are available for download on the AccountAbility website.

[16] For further discussion of AA1000SES (2015), see A. Gutterman, *Stakeholders and Stakeholder Engagement* (Oakland CA: Sustainable Entrepreneurship Project, 2019) available at www.seproject.org.

accountable, responsible, and sustainable, and address issues affecting governance, business models, and organizational strategy.

AA1000AP (2018), which is the foundation of the AccountAbility series of standards, is based on four fundamental principles[17]:

- *Impact:* Impact is the effect of behavior, performance, and/ or outcomes, on the part of individuals or an organization, on the economy, the environment, society, stakeholders, or the organization itself. Organizations have a responsibility to monitor, measure, and be accountable for how their action affect their broader ecosystems and the principle of impact is of central importance to the accountability process and supports the interactions among the other fundamental principles.
- *Materiality:* Decision makers need to identify and be clear about the sustainability topics that matter most to their organizations and stakeholders. In order to do this, attention needs to be paid to the principle of materiality, which relates to identifying and prioritizing the most relevant sustainability topics, taking into account the effect each topic has on an organization and its stakeholders. AA1000AP (2018) explains that a material topic is a topic that will substantively influence and impact the assessments, decisions, actions, and performance of an organization and/or its stakeholders in the short, medium, and/or long term.
- *Inclusivity:* According to AA1000AP (2018), people should have a say in the decisions that impact them and this means that organizations need to embrace the principle of inclusivity by actively identifying stakeholders and enabling their participation in establishing the organization's material sustainability topics and developing a strategic response to them. Inclusive organizations accept their accountability to

---

[17] The descriptions of the four principles are adapted from AA1000 AccountAbility Principles (2018), 13 and 30.

those on whom they have an impact and to those who have an impact on them.

- *Responsiveness:* AA1000AP (2018) describes responsiveness as an organization's timely and relevant reaction to material sustainability topics and their related impacts. Organizations should be prepared to act transparently on these topics and impacts and demonstrate responsiveness through their decisions, actions, and performance, as well as their communications with stakeholders.

British Standard on Sustainability Management, BS 8900

The British Standard on Sustainability Management, referred to as "BS 8900," was first published in May 2006 by BSI (www.bsigroup.com) for use in independently auditing, verifying, and certifying an organization's sustainable development strategy and a fully revised version was issued in August 2013. Part I of BS 8900 contains guidance on principles of sustainable development such as inclusivity, integrity, stewardship, and transparency and how those principles can be embedded in organizations. Part II of BS 8900 sets out the framework for assessing an organization's approach to sustainable development. The drafters of BS 8900 emphasized that it was not designed to duplicate existing management systems specifications, such as ISO 9001 or ISO 14001, but was intended to optimize the value of existing approaches. BS 8900 was developed for the consultants and managers responsible for sustainability within an organization, including the CEO and senior executives responsible for sustainability, compliance, corporate social responsibility, and environment.

Committee on Sustainability Assessment

The Committee on Sustainability Assessment (COSA) (thecosa.org) is a neutral, nonprofit consortium dedicated to fostering innovative and pragmatic systems that accelerate sustainability. COSA uses the principles of collaboration and partnership to identify solid standardized metrics about what is "sustainable" in order to provide sustainability intelligence and advance sustainability by providing organizations, governments, and businesses with the ability to speak a common sustainability "language" of accountability in the same way that we have generally accepted accounting principles to understand finance. COSA has developed and field-tested state-of-the-art metrics for economic, social, and environmental indicators in collaboration with more than 60 global partners and hundreds of institutions and experts. COSA metrics are benchmarked to dozens of international norms and accords including the Sustainable Development Goals, multilateral guidelines, international agreements, and normative references. Corporations, financial institutions, and government agencies use COSA metrics and technologies to improve services and target smarter investments, and COSA has emerged as a trusted source for sustainability intelligence and tools that are aligned with dozens of international accords. COSA's experience began with coffee, the world's most economically important agricultural commodity, and now includes cocoa, cotton, sugar, tea, field crops, fruit and food crops. COSA works primarily in developing countries and across global agri-food supply chains.[18]

ISO 9001

ISO 9001 is one of the best known and widely used standards of the ISO and provides a structure (i.e., a quality management system (QMS)) to help organizations develop products and services that consistently ensure customer satisfaction and continuously improve their products, services, and process. Quality refers to all those features of a product or service that are required by the customer. Quality management means what an organization does to ensure that its products or services satisfy the customer's quality requirements and comply with any regulations applicable to those products or services. Quality management also means what the organization does to enhance customer satisfaction and achieve continual improvement of its performance. ISO 9001 gives the requirements for what the organization must do to manage processes affecting the quality of its final products and services; however, ISO 9001 is not a

---

[18] For further discussion of COSA tools and methodology, see Giovannucci, D., O. von Hagen, and J. Wozniak. 2014. "Corporate Social Responsibility and the Role of Voluntary Sustainability Standards." In *Voluntary Standards Systems,* eds. Schmitz-Hoffmann, et al., 359, 375–381 Berlin: Springer-Verlag.

product or service standard, nor does it specify what the objectives of the organization should be with respect to "quality" or "meeting customer requirements," each of which must be defined by organizations on their own.

ISO 14001

ISO 14001 is an internationally agreed standard developed by ISO that sets out the requirements for a structure (i.e., an environmental management system (EMS)) to help organizations manage and minimize their environmental impacts, conform to applicable legal requirements, and improve their environmental performance through more efficient use of resources and reduction of waste, thereby gaining a competitive advantage and the trust of stakeholders. ISO 14001, which was recently revised effective in 2015, is suitable for organizations of all types and sizes, be they private, not-for-profit or governmental, and requires that an organization consider all environmental issues relevant to its operations, such as air pollution, water and sewage issues, waste management, soil contamination, climate change mitigation and adaptation, and resource use and efficiency. While an EMS may be adopted as a standalone system, it is often added to an existing management system (e.g., a system based on quality, such as ISO 9001 described earlier).

ISO 26000

ISO 26000:2010 provides guidance to all types of organizations, regardless of their size or location, on concepts, terms, and definitions related to social responsibility; the background, trends and characteristics of social responsibility; principles and practices relating to social responsibility; the core subjects and issues of social responsibility; integrating, implementing, and promoting socially responsible behavior throughout the organization and, through its policies and practices, within its sphere of influence; identifying and engaging with stakeholders; and communicating commitments, performance, and other information related to social responsibility. ISO 26000 defines "social responsibility" as the responsibility of an organization for the impacts of its decisions and activities (i.e., products, services, and processes) on society and the environment through transparent and ethical behavior that contributes to sustainable development, including the health and welfare of society; takes into account the expectations of stakeholders; is in compliance with applicable law and consistent with international norms of behavior, and is integrated throughout the organization and practiced in its relationships, which includes all of the organization's activities within its sphere of influence (i.e., relationships through which the organization has the ability to affect the decisions or activities of others).

The specific clauses of ISO 26000 can be described as follows: Clause title, Clause n°, Description of clause contents

- Clause 1 defines the scope of ISO 26000 and identifies certain limitations and exclusions.
- Clause 2 identifies and provides the definition of key terms that are of fundamental importance for understanding social responsibility and for using ISO 26000.
- Clause 3 describes the important factors and conditions that have influenced the development of social responsibility and that continue to affect its nature and practice. It also describes the concept of social responsibility itself: what it means and how it applies to organizations. The clause includes guidance for small and medium-sized organizations on the use of ISO 26000.
- Clause 4 introduces and explains the principles of social responsibility: accountability, transparency, ethical behavior, respect for stakeholder interests, respect for the rule of law, respect for international norms of behavior, and respect for human rights.
- Clause 5 addresses two practices of social responsibility: an organization's recognition of its social responsibility, and its identification of, and engagement with, its stakeholders. It provides guidance on the relationship between an organization, its stakeholders and society, on recognizing the core subjects and issues of social responsibility, and on an organization's sphere of influence.

- Clause 6 explains the core subjects and associated issues relating to social responsibility including organizational governance, human rights, labor practices, the environment, fair operating practices, consumer issues, and community involvement and development. For each core subject, information is provided on its scope, including key issues; its relationship to social responsibility; related principles and considerations; and related actions and expectations.

- Clause 7 provides guidance on putting social responsibility into practice in an organization. This includes understanding the social responsibility of an organization, integrating social responsibility throughout an organization, communication related to social responsibility, improving the credibility of an organization regarding social responsibility, reviewing progress, and improving performance and evaluating voluntary initiatives for social responsibility. This involves making social responsibility integral to its policies, organizational culture, strategies and operations; building internal competency for social responsibility; undertaking internal and external communication on social responsibility; and regularly reviewing these actions and practices related to social responsibility.

ISO 26000:2010 is intended to assist organizations in contributing to sustainable development; however, although it draws on principles included in the management systems developed by the ISO it is not itself a management system standard and is not intended or appropriate for certification purposes or regulatory or contractual use.[19] Instead, ISO 26000:2010 sets out certain core principles and explains the core subjects and associated issues relating to social responsibility including organizational governance, human rights, labor practices, the environment, fair operating practices, consumer issues, and community involvement

---

[19] See International Organization for Standardization, ISO 26000 Guidance on Social Responsibility: Discovering ISO 26000 (2014) and *Handbook for Implementers of ISO 26000, Global Guidance Standard on Social Responsibility by Small and Medium Sized Businesses* (Middlebury, VT: ECOLOGIA, 2011).

and development. For each core subject, information is provided on its scope, including key issues; its relationship to social responsibility; related principles and considerations; and related actions and expectations. For example, with respect to labor practices, one of the core subjects, organizations are reminded to integrate consideration of the following issues into their policies, organizational culture, strategies, and operations: employment and employment relationships; conditions of work and social protection; social dialogue; health and safety at work; and human development and training in the workplace.[20]

The seven principles of ISO 26000:2010 are intended to establish the underlying framework for socially responsible decision making and link each user of ISO 26000:2010 to a global community of those who share the following principles:

- *Accountability:* Accountability is the state of being answerable for decisions and activities to the organization's governing bodies, legal authorities and, more broadly, its stakeholders (i.e., those who are affected by the actions of the organization)
- *Transparency:* Transparency is openness about decisions and activities that affect society, the economy and the environment, and willingness to communicate these in a clear, accurate, timely, honest, and complete manner.
- *Ethical Behavior:* Ethical behavior involves deciding on the right course of action, day to day, and is defined as "behavior that is in accordance with accepted principles of right or good conduct in the context of a particular situation."

---

[20] ISO 26000 Guidance on Social Responsibility: Discovering ISO 26000 (International Organization for Standardization, 2014) and *Handbook for Implementers of ISO 26000, Global Guidance Standard on Social Responsibility by Small and Medium Sized Businesses* (Middlebury, VT: ECOLOGIA, 2011). The discussion of ISO 26000 in this section is adapted from ISO 26000 Basic Training Manual (ISO 26000 Post Publication Organization, March 15, 2016). ISO 26000 is available for purchase from ISO webstore at the ISO website (www.iso.org) and general information about ISO 26000 can be obtained at www.iso.org/sr

- *Respect for Stakeholder Interests:* Respect for stakeholder interests requires identifying groups of stakeholders (i.e., those who are affected by the decisions and actions of the organization), understanding the impact of the organization's decisions and actions on those stakeholders, and responding to their concerns, although this does not mean that stakeholders should be allowed to make decisions for the organization.
- *Respect for the Rule of Law:* In the context of social responsibility, respect for the rule of law means that an organization complies with all applicable laws and regulations, even if they are not adequately enforced.
- *Respect for International Norms of Behavior:* In situations where the law or its implementation does not provide for adequate environmental or social safeguards, an organization should strive to respect, as a minimum, international norms of behavior, which are derived from customary international law, generally accepted principles of international law, or intergovernmental agreements that are universally or nearly universally recognized.
- *Respect for Human Rights:* Organizations should identify the vulnerable populations among its stakeholders and work to ensure their fair treatment including, in situations where human rights are not protected, taking steps to respect human rights and avoid taking advantage of these situations.

OHSAS 18001: Occupational Health and Safety Management

BS OHSAS 18001 sets out the minimum requirements for occupational health and safety management best practice and provides a framework for an occupational health and safety management system that can be used to put in place the policies, procedures, and controls needed for an organization to achieve the best possible working conditions and workplace health and safety, aligned to internationally recognized best practice.

Social Accountability International

Social Accountability International (SAI) (sa-intl.org) is a global NGO advancing human rights at work driven by diverse perspectives to navigating evolving labor issues. SAI's vision is of decent work everywhere, sustained by an understanding that socially responsible workplaces benefit business while securing fundamental human rights. SAI empowers workers and managers at all levels of businesses and supply chains, using its multiindustry SA8000® Standard, which is the leading social certification standard for factories and organizations across the globe. SA8000 measures social performance in eight areas important to social accountability in workplaces (i.e., child labor, forced or compulsory labor, health and safety, freedom of association and right to collective bargaining, discrimination, disciplinary practices, working hours and remuneration), anchored by a management system element that drives continuous improvement in all areas of the Standard. The Standard reflects labor provisions contained within the Universal Declaration of Human Rights and ILO conventions, and also respects, complements and supports national labor laws around the world. As of September 2019, the Standard was being used in over 4,200 factories across 62 countries and 56 industries and was helping secure ethical working conditions for over two million workers.[21]

In addition to publishing SA8000 and supporting documents, SAI offers a wide selection of resources to help organizations maintain and continually improve their social performance, including capacity building, stakeholder engagement, collaboration between buyers and suppliers, and the development of tools to ensure continued improvement. SAI views independent accredited certification to the SA8000® Standard as a critical element contributing to the company's broader objectives of improving global labor conditions. SAI is also one of the world's leading social compliance training organizations, having provided training to over 30,000 people, including factory and farm managers, workers, brand compliance officers, auditors, labor inspectors, trade union representatives, and other worker rights advocates.

---

[21] Current information on certification and accreditation can be obtained at http://saasaccreditation.org/

CHAPTER 5

Securities Exchanges and Regulators

Governments play a variety of roles in the financial system including enforcing disclosure rules and norms that facilitate the transfer of information by those in need of capital to those will to provide capital in order to ensure that capital providers are able to make informed decisions about whether to invest or lend. One of the ways in which regulators intervene in the capital-raising process is through the imposition of rules relating to corporate governance. While corporate governance has traditionally focused on the creation of value for the owners an enterprise, the emergence of corporate social responsibility (CSR) has expanded the scope of the corporate governance framework to include consideration of the interests of a wider group of stakeholders. These changes in the conceptualization of corporate governance are beginning to impact expectations regarding operations and disclosures that are imposed on companies that seek funding in capital markets and continuous attention must be paid to standards and rules adopted by securities exchanges and the governmental bodies that regulate them.[1]

---

[1] In some countries, notably in Europe, companies may also be guided in their governance activities by voluntary codes of conduct relating to corporate governance that are actually reviewed and formally endorsed by governments in those countries. In some cases, the governance provisions are made mandatory through incorporation into national company laws. CSR is fundamentally a corporate governance topic and the OECD has explained that in dealing with corporate governance issues, countries use various combinations of legal and regulatory instruments on the one hand, and codes and principles on the other. For example, in all OECD jurisdictions, corporate governance standards are included in company law and securities law. Company laws set forth the default option concerning corporate structures whose detailed framework is determined by the

While the public securities markets in the United States remain the largest and deepest in the world, there is clearly competition from other markets that are achieving extremely high levels of growth including capital markets in the Eurozone, the Asia-Pacific region, and in emerging markets such as China and India, and securities exchanges and regulatory authorities in these jurisdictions have often shown global leadership in integrating corporate governance and CSR. In general, regulation has focused on disclosure rather than compliance with explicit standards relating to environmental and/or social actions. According to a report issued by the Hauser Center, as of 2015, 23 countries had enacted legislation since 2000 to require companies to issue reports that included environmental and/or social information.[2] A 2016 report compiled by KPMG, GRI, UNEP, and the Centre for Corporate Governance in Africa noted that governments around the world had introduced a number of mandatory reporting instruments and that as a result of the level of activity in ESG reporting over 80 percent of the world's top economies by GDP in 2016 mandated ESG reporting in some form.[3]

---

company's articles and bylaws, and securities laws set forth binding requirements, making shareholder protection enforceable for regulators. A few jurisdictions (e.g., India and the United States) do not have national codes or principles under the "comply or explain" framework and instead rely on laws and regulations (including listing rules) as the main framework for addressing corporate governance issues. See *OECD Corporate Governance Fact Book* (2017).

[2] Williams, C. 2016. "Corporate Social Responsibility and Corporate Governance." In *Oxford Handbook of Corporate Law and Governance,* eds. J. Gordon and G. Ringe, 15–16. Oxford: Oxford University Press, available at http://digital commons.osgoode.yorku.ca/scholarly_works/1784 (citing Initiative for Responsible Investment, Corporate Social Responsibility Disclosure Efforts by National Governments and Stock Exchanges (March 12, 2015), available at http://hauser center.org/iri/wpcontent/uploads/2011/08/CR-3-12-15.pdf and noting that countries included Argentina, China, Denmark, the EU, Ecuador, Finland, France, Germany Greece, Hungary, India, Indonesia, Ireland, Italy, Japan, Malaysia, The Netherlands, Norway, South Africa, Spain, Sweden, Taiwan, and the UK).

[3] The 2016 "Carrots & Sticks" Report, https://assets.kpmg.com/ content/dam/ kpmg/pdf/2016/05/ carrots-and-sticks-may-2016.pdf

United States

In the United States, the process of raising capital through the offer and sale of securities is strictly controlled at the federal level through the regulatory framework laid out in the provisions of the Securities Act of 1933, as amended (Securities Act) and the Exchange Act of 1934, as amended (Exchange Act). The focus of the Securities Act is the disclosures and liabilities involved in the offer and sale of securities to the investment community, in both private and public offerings. Under Section 5 of the Securities Act, offers and sales of securities must be registered with the Securities and Exchange Commission (SEC) unless one of the exemptions from registration included in Sections 3 and 4 of the Securities Act is available. Disclosures in the registration statement are intended to include all of the material information regarding the issuer and the terms of the offering and the Securities Act contains provisions designed to insure that the information is widely disseminated to the members of the investment community before the offering is completed.

The basic purposes of the Exchange Act are to regulate securities exchanges and the securities market; to make available to persons who buy and sell securities information relating to the issuers of such securities; to prevent fraud in securities trading and manipulation of markets; and to control the amount of credit which may be used in the securities market. The provisions of the Exchange Act relate primarily to the activities of issuers and their affiliates after their securities have been distributed into the public market; however, the Exchange Act also establishes a number of rules relating to the creation and operation of the securities markets, including requirements applicable to stock exchanges and their listing standards. Many of rules that regulate the corporate governance practices of companies subject to Exchange Act requirements are effectively imposed through the listing standards of the major U.S. national securities exchanges—the New York Stock Exchange (NYSE) and The Nasdaq Stock Market (Nasdaq)—with respect to disclosure and protection of shareholder rights. The requirements of the two exchanges differ in some respects; however, each has adopted both quantitative and qualitative standards. Corporate governance-related listing criteria include the independence of directors, audit committee requirements, requirements for compensation and nominating committees to minimize or resolve conflicts of interest, and voting rights and shareholder approval requirements.

In contrast to Europe, the United States has been slower in using formal regulation to incorporate CSR into the business strategies and operations of corporations, an approach that is consistent with the preference in the United States for minimal legislative control of business, and has instead emphasized developing specialized organizations that set rules and standards, and provide enforcement regimes, for certain aspects of CSR including the Occupational Safety and Health Administration, Equal Employment Opportunity Commission, Consumer Product Safety Commission, and the Environmental Protection Agency.[4] Areas in which the SEC has engaged in rule-making, often with middling success due to legal challenges, or issuance of guidance on disclosures have included disclosures of environmental litigation against any government agency where a penalty of $100,000 is sought; explanation of climate risks to their future profitability, either from physical changes associated with climate change, or from regulatory initiatives designed to mitigate climate risk; disclosure of the ratio of the CEO's total pay to the median employee pay; mine safety disclosure; "conflict minerals" disclosure where tin; tantalum, tungsten, or gold from the Democratic Republic of the Congo or neighboring countries were incorporated into listed companies' products; and "publish what you pay" transparency disclosure for extractive company payments to host countries.[5]

---

[4] Rahim, M. 2013. *Legal Regulation of Corporate Social Responsibility: A Meta-Regulation Approach of Law for Raising CSR in a Weak Economy*, 13, 38–39. Berlin: Springer.

[5] Williams, C. 2016. "Corporate Social Responsibility and Corporate Governance." In *Oxford Handbook of Corporate Law and Governance*, eds. J. Gordon and G. Ringe, 17–18. Oxford: Oxford University Press, available at http://digitalcommons.osgoode.yorku.ca/scholarly_works/1784. Several of the topics were placed on the agenda as part of the Dodd-Frank Wall Street Reform and Consumer Protection Act of 2010; however, the rules relating to "conflict minerals" disclosure and "publish what you pay" drew strong challenges from the National Association of Manufacturers and the American Petroleum Institute and, in fact, attempts to enforce "publish what you pay" have effectively been abandoned by the SEC.

United Kingdom

Many aspects of securities regulation in the UK are overseen by the Financial Conduct Authority (www.fca.org.uk) and the London Stock Exchange (LSE) (www.londonstockexchange.com) is the main securities exchange in the UK and one of the leading global markets. The UK established a post of CSR Minister to encourage greater social responsibility in UK companies and the UK's Companies Act of 2006 includes specific reporting requirements on environmental and social issues.[6] The LSE is one of a growing number of stock exchanges that now requires social and/or environmental disclosure as part of its listing requirements.[7] Premium companies listed on the LSE's Main Market, its highest level, have been required to subscribe to the principles laid down in the UK Corporate Governance Code, which sets out methods for best practice corporate governance, or must provide an explanation of why they do not, and rules changes adopted by the LSE to take effect at the end of September 2018 require companies traded on its AIM Market for smaller growth companies to adopt a recognized corporate governance code. While AIM-traded companies are free to follow the UK Corporate Governance Code in full or in part, the new rules provide flexibility by allowing boards to choose any "recognized" code including the Quoted Companies Alliance (QCA)

---

[6] Rahim, M. Springer, 2013. *Legal Regulation of Corporate Social Responsibility: A Meta-Regulation Approach of Law for Raising CSR in a Weak Economy*, 13, 34–38, Berlin. Williams, C. 2016. "Corporate Social Responsibility and Corporate Governance." In *Oxford Handbook of Corporate Law and Governance*, Gordon, J., and G. Ringe, 14–15. Oxford: Oxford University Press, available at http://digitalcommons.osgoode.yorku.ca/scholarly_works/1784.

[7] Williams, C. 2016. "Corporate Social Responsibility and Corporate Governance." In *Oxford Handbook of Corporate Law and Governance*, eds. J. Gordon and G. Ringe, 15–16. Oxford: Oxford University Press. available at http://digitalcommons.osgoode.yorku.ca/scholarly_works/1784 (citing Initiative for Responsible Investment, Corporate Social Responsibility Disclosure Efforts by National Governments and Stock Exchanges (March 12, 2015), available at http://hausercenter.org/iri/wpcontent/uploads/2011/08/CR-3-12-15.pdf).

Corporate Governance Code[8] or an overseas code (e.g., when a company is admitted to another market it may be easier and more appropriate for it to comply to standards imposed in its home jurisdiction). AIM-traded companies will be expected to ensure that they provide meaningful information so that investors can understand their approach to corporate governance.

LSE has issued guidance setting out recommendations for good practice in ESG reporting.[9] LSE noted that the governance and reporting framework in the UK encourages reporting of ESG and nonfinancial matters through the Guidance on the Strategic Report and Corporate Governance Code requirements for disclosure of principal risks and uncertainties and a viability statement, and pointed out 2013 updates to the UK Companies Act 2006 included a number of ESG reporting provisions. For example, companies incorporated in the UK that have listed securities (i.e., those with equity shares listed on LSE Main Market, EEA regulated, NYSE, or NASDAQ) are expected to explain how they are managing issues such as environmental performance, human rights, social and community involvement, and diversity, and are also expected to report on certain statistics (e.g., Scope 1 and 2 CO_2 emissions and gender diversity at board, senior management, and whole-company levels). Requirements differ for companies of different sizes and listed status.[10]

European Union

Global companies in Europe have been guided by the EU Commission's Green Paper on Promoting a Framework for CSR and the European

---

[8] A variety of publications for small- and medium-sized companies listed on the LSE are available on the QCA website (http://theqca.com/shop/guides/) including guides to reporting and the operations of the audit and various other board committees.

[9] *Revealing the Full Picture: Your Guide to ESG Reporting.* (London Stock Exchange Group, January 2018), https://lseg.com/sites/default/files/content/images/Green_Finance/ESG/2018/February/LSEG_ESG_report_January_2018.pdf

[10] Id. at 34–35.

Code of Conduct Regarding the Activities of Transnational Corporations Operating in Developing Economies.[11] Since 2003 EU accounting rules as stated in the EU Accounts Modernization Directive have required companies to report on environmental and labor issues "to the extent necessary" to provide investors with an accurate view of the company's financial position and the risks to that position.[12] An EU Directive that entered into force on December 6, 2014, attempted to establish a minimum standard for ESG reporting throughout the EU by requiring new national legislation to be adopted by the Member States within two years that obligates approximately 6,000 large companies and "public interest organizations," such as banks and insurance companies, to "prepare a nonfinancial statement containing information relating to at least environmental matters, social and employee-related matters, respect for human rights, anti-corruption, and bribery matters."[13] There is a further requirement for quoted companies to either include a description of their diversity policy and how it has been implemented or to explain why one is not relevant.[14]

A number of individual countries in Europe have also taken action driven, at least in part, by a series of resolutions adopted by the European Parliament to facilitate the development of the incorporation of CSR principles in its member economies such as, for example, requiring that

---

[11] For further information, see http://ec.europa.eu/growth/industry/corporate-social-responsibility_en

[12] Williams, C. 2016. "Corporate Social Responsibility and Corporate Governance." In *Oxford Handbook of Corporate Law and Governance*, eds. J. Gordon and G. Ringe, 14. Oxford: Oxford University Press, Available at http://digitalcommons.osgoode.yorku.ca/scholarly_works/1784.

[13] See Directive 2014/95/EU of the European Parliament and of the Council of October 22, 2014, amending Directive 2013/34/EU as regards disclosure of nonfinancial and diversity information by certain large undertakings and groups, Official Journal of the European Union L330/1-330/9

[14] *Revealing the Full Picture: Your Guide to ESG Reporting* (London Stock Exchange Group, January 2018), 34-35, https://lseg.com/sites/default/files/content/images/Green_Finance/ESG/2018/February/LSEG_ESG_report_January_2018.pdf

companies adopt "triple bottom line" reporting on their environmental and social performance: Belgium passed legislation requiring pension fund managers to disclose the extent to which they consider ethical, social, and environmental criteria in their investment policies and legislation requiring companies to report on social performance, although companies have not been forced to adhere to and comply with specific ILO conventions; France requires listed companies to disclose their impact on social and environmental issues in their annual reports and accounts; Germany requires public companies to issue reports including environmental and/or social information; and each of the Scandinavian countries have mandated publication of sustainability reports by public companies that are consistent with widely recognized frameworks such as the GRI and the UN Global Compact and which are expected to address labor issues, human rights concerns, gender equality, antidiscrimination, and environmental issues.[15]

Various countries in Europe, in the course of making recommendation in their national corporate governance codes, have recommended that companies adopt policies on CSR that include a determination and statement of the company's values and ethical guidelines to be followed in accordance with such values; include information about the environment and its impact on financial performance in their financial reports; disclose various risk factors, including environmental risks; establish risk management systems that cover ethical risks; disclose information to and about stakeholders and enable communications between stakeholders and the company's supervisory body; involve stakeholders in the development and implementation of CSR practices; establish requirements that candidates for board membership should have adequate personal integrity and business ethics; and adopt ethical policies and continuously train

---

[15] Rahim, M. 2013. *Legal Regulation of Corporate Social Responsibility: A Meta-Regulation Approach of Law for Raising CSR in a Weak Economy*, 13, 34–38. Berlin: Springer; Williams, C. 2016. "Corporate Social Responsibility and Corporate Governance." In *Oxford Handbook of Corporate Law and Governance*, eds. J. Gordon and G. Ringe, 14–15. Oxford: Oxford University Press. Available at http://digitalcommons.osgoode.yorku.ca/scholarly_works/1784

employees on the principles in those policies.[16] There have also been a number of important quasi-legal initiatives for the promotion of CSR at the national level throughout Europe including the International Business Leaders Forum, the Ethical Trading Initiative, and Partnership for Global Responsibility.[17]

Germany

Securities markets in Germany are separated by law into two different markets which differ in terms of their approach to regulation of trading, listing, and ongoing obligations.[18] The first market is the "Regulated Market," which is the most regulated market in terms of listing requirements and ongoing obligations, and the second market is the "Regulated Unofficial Market." The segmentation into two markets applies to all of the stock exchanges in Germany, which include multiple stock exchanges based in various financial centers (the Frankfurt Stock Exchange is the main stock exchange in Germany), the electronic stock exchange "Eurex" for futures transactions, a commodities exchange in Hannover and energy exchanges in Frankfurt and Leipzig. National oversight of all German securities markets and providers of financial and

---

[16] Szabó, D., and K. Sørensen. 2013. "Integrating Corporate Social Responsibility in Corporate Governance Codes in the EU." *European Business Law Review* 6, no. 1, pp. 20–32. Only 10 of the codes expressly referred to CSR or social responsibility and only a few of the codes attempted to clarify or define the term. Definitions were usually quite general, such as the company's responsibility for the manner in which its activities affect people, society, and the environment. Norway's code offered examples of issues that might be covered by CSR such as human rights, prevention of corruption, employee rights, health and safety, and the working environment, and discrimination, as well as environmental issues.

[17] Rahim, M. 2013. *Legal Regulation of Corporate Social Responsibility: A Meta-Regulation Approach of Law for Raising CSR in a Weak Economy*, 13, 34–38. Berlin: Springer.

[18] Portions of the discussion of the discussion of securities regulation in Germany in this section are adapted from Kurth, M., and O. Rothley. 2010. "Securities Law in Germany." In *International Securities Law Handbook*, 3rd ed. The Netherlands: Kluwer Law International.

securities trading services is provided by the Federal Financial Supervisory Authority (BaFin). The operation of securities markets in Germany is subject to a wide range of laws and regulations including the Stock Exchange Act, which sets out basic principles regarding the organization of stock exchanges and other securities markets and the trading and list of securities; the Stock Exchange Admission Regulation, which sets out listing requirements, listing procedures, and disclosure obligations for securities for which an application for admission to the Regulated Market has been filed or will be filed; and the Securities Trading Act, which focuses on the regulation of trading with securities, financial instruments, futures, derivatives, and similar financial products and addresses a number of important areas such as disclosure of changes of interests in stock of listed corporations, preparation and distribution of annual and quarterly financial reports, proxy and voting procedures, and insider trading. Germany was one of the first countries in which legislation was enacted requiring public companies to issue reports including environmental and/or social information and the new EU requirements have been adopted and implemented in Germany through the German CSR Directive Implementation Act.[19] The German Sustainability Code, an initiative driven by the German Council for Sustainable Development, provides a comprehensive framework for reporting nonfinancial information that addresses topics in areas such as strategy, process management, environmental matters, and society.

France

Securities regulation in France falls to the Autorite des Marches Financiers (AMF), which was established in 2003 under France's Financial

---

[19] Williams, C. 2016. "Corporate Social Responsibility and Corporate Governance." In *Oxford Handbook of Corporate Law and Governance*, eds. J. Gordon and G. Ringe, 1516. Oxford: Oxford University Press, Available at http://digitalcommons.osgoode.yorku.ca/scholarly_works/1784 (citing Initiative for Responsible Investment, Corporate Social Responsibility Disclosure Efforts by National Governments and Stock Exchanges (March 12, 2015), available at http://hausercenter.org/iri/wpcontent/uploads/2011/08/CR-3-12-15.pdf).

Security Act of August 1, 2003.[20] The AMF is intended to be an independent public authority that is responsible for regulating and policing French financial markets in order to protect savings and investment. The AMF has statutory responsibility for safeguarding investment in financial products, ensuring that investors receive material information and maintaining orderly markets. Corporate financing is an important area of responsibility for the AMF and all listed firms are required to inform the public regularly regarding their business activities and results and about major transactions such as capital increases and rights issues, tender and exchange offers, and takeovers and mergers. The AMF oversees the preparation and disclosure of financial and other business information regarding listed firms to ensure that such information is accurate, true, fair, and timely and properly disseminated throughout the entire financial community. France was the first country in Europe to enact legislation requiring public companies to issue reports including environmental and/or social information, beginning in 2002 with a requirement that listed companies report data on 40 labor and social criteria and then expanding requirements in 2009 to mandate publication of greenhouse gas emission by companies with more than 500 employees in high-emitting sectors.[21] Hosting the Paris Climate Conference in 2015 has been a source of great pride for environmental and social activists in France and it has been predicted that France will continue to move forward aggressively toward become the world leader in "green financing" and nurturing the development of "best practices" sustainable companies.

---

[20] Portions of the discussion of the Autorite des Marches Financiers in this section are adapted from material found at www.amf-france.org.

[21] Williams, C. 2016. "Corporate Social Responsibility and Corporate Governance." In *Oxford Handbook of Corporate Law and Governance*, eds. J. Gordon and G. Ringe, 1516. Oxford: Oxford University Press, Available at http://digitalcommons.osgoode.yorku.ca/scholarly_works/1784 (citing Initiative for Responsible Investment, Corporate Social Responsibility Disclosure Efforts by National Governments and Stock Exchanges (March 12, 2015), available at http://hausercenter.org/iri/wpcontent/uploads/2011/08/CR-3-12-15.pdf).

Japan

Principles of CSR have been important in Japan since the postwar reconstruction period, during which the resolution "Awareness and Practice of the Social Responsibility of Business" was adopted and stated the fundamental principle that businesses should not simply pursue corporate profit, but must seek harmony between the economy and society, combining factors of products and services, and that social responsibility is a better way to pursue this goal.[22] Various cabinet ministries have undertaken initiatives to promote and achieve CSR including the Cabinet Office; the Ministry of Agriculture, Forestry, and Fisheries; the Ministry of Health, Labor, and Welfare; and the Ministry of Environment. For example, the Cabinet Office issued its "Corporate Code of Conduct" in 2002 to build consumer confidence in businesses and set guidelines to promote the establishment and implementation of corporate codes of conduct.[23] The influential Ministry of Economy, Trade, and Industry collaborated with the Japanese Standards Association on the creation of a working group to develop CSR standards in Japan and Japan has been an active participant in the development of intergovernmental initiatives relating to CSR. The result of all this activity has been that Japanese companies have been global leaders in disclosures of CSR activities, investment in internal resources to oversee CSR commitments and adoption of codes of conduct based on international standards.[24]

The Financial Instruments and Exchange Law (FIEL) regulates stocks and securities in Japan and requires registration for "sales and solicitation" operations of securities and derivative transactions. Among other things, the FIEL mandate quarterly reporting for listed companies, who

---

[22] Rahim, M. 2013. *Legal Regulation of Corporate Social Responsibility: A Meta-Regulation Approach of Law for Raising CSR in a Weak Economy*, 1340. Berlin: Springer, (citing Kawamura, M. 2004. *The Evolution of Corporate Social Responsibility in Japan (Part 1)—Parallels with the History of Corporate Reform, 156.* NLI Research institute.

[23] Id. (citing Asian Productivity Organisation, Policies to Promote Corporate Social Responsibility (Report of the Asian Productivity Organisation Top Management Forum, 2006)).

[24] Id. at 41–42.

are subject to audits by certified public accountants or auditing firms and subject to criminal or civil penalties for submitting false quarterly reports; mandate internal control reports to ensure appropriate disclosure of financial and corporate information; and require submissions of certifications by management of listed companies stating that the descriptions in their financial statements are appropriate and in compliance with laws and regulations.

Japan is one of the countries in which legislation has been enacted requiring public companies to issue reports including environmental and/ or social information; however, the emphasis among Japanese companies has traditionally leaned toward environmental matters with social issues being considered as less important.[25] Japan has been slowly moving forward with corporate governance reforms intended to make Japanese companies and markets more competitive globally. The Council of Experts Concerning the Corporate Governance Code—Japan Financial Services Agency stated on March 5, 2015: "It is important the companies operate themselves with the full recognition of responsibilities to a range of stakeholders, starting with fiduciary responsibility to shareholders who have entrusted the management. The Code seeks "growth-oriented governance promoting timely and decisive decision making based upon transparent and fair decision making through the fulfillment of companies' accountability in relating to responsibilities to shareholders and stakeholders."[26] In 2015 Japan's governance code was amended to require a minimum of two independent directors and encourage companies to consider at least one-third independent boards and boost the number of female directors. Japan has a long way to go on those subjects with surveys

---

[25] Williams, C. 2016. "Corporate Social Responsibility and Corporate Governance." In *Oxford Handbook of Corporate Law and Governance*, eds. J. Gordon and G. Ringe, 15–16. Oxford: Oxford University Press, Available at http:// digitalcommons.osgoode.yorku.ca/scholarly_works/1784 (citing Initiative for Responsible Investment, Corporate Social Responsibility Disclosure Efforts by National Governments and Stock Exchanges (March 12, 2015), available at http://hausercenter.org/iri/wpcontent/uploads/2011/08/CR-3-12-15.pdf).

[26] Japan's Corporate Governance Overhaul (Bloomberg Intelligence, January 6, 2017), https://bloomberg.com/professional/blog/japans-corporate-governance-overhaul-2/

showing that Nikkei 225 companies have the lowest median proportion of independent directors and female directors and the oldest average age among developed-market peers.[27]

China

China's stock market is comprised of two stock exchanges, the Shanghai Stock Exchange (www.sse.com.cn) (SSE), established in 1990, and the Shenzhen Stock Exchange (www.szse.cn) (SZSE), established in 1991, and responsibility for regulatory oversight is vested in the China Securities Regulatory Commission (www.csrc.gov.cn). China is one of the countries in which legislation has been enacted requiring public companies to issue reports including environmental and/or social information.[28] In 2006, the SZSE released the Guidelines on Social Responsibilities of Companies Listed at the Shenzhen Stock Exchange, under which listed companies were required to actively protect the legitimate rights and interests of debtors and employees while pursuing economic benefits and protecting shareholder interests; treat suppliers, customers, and consumers with good faith; take an active part in environmental protection, community development, and other public causes; and develop a balanced and harmonious relationship with the communities. Listed companies were encouraged to develop social responsibility systems, conduct regular inspection, and assessment of the progress made in implementing the systems and issues to be addressed, and regularly draft and release reports on social responsibilities. In 2008 the SSE issued the Notice on Enhancing CSR Requirements for Listed Companies, which emphasized the

---

[27] Id.

[28] Williams, C. 2016. "Corporate Social Responsibility and Corporate Governance." In *Oxford Handbook of Corporate Law and Governance*, eds. J. Gordon and G. Ringe,15–16. Oxford: Oxford University Press, available at http://digitalcommons.osgoode.yorku.ca/scholarly_works/1784 (citing Initiative for Responsible Investment, Corporate Social Responsibility Disclosure Efforts by National Governments and Stock Exchanges (March 12, 2015), available at http://hausercenter.org/iri/wpcontent/uploads/2011/08/CR-3-12-15.pdf).

noncommercial contribution by stakeholders, society, environmental protection, and resource uses, and encouraged listed companies to disclose its special practices and achievements in CSR delivery and release its annual CSR report along with its annual report.[29] However, while sustainability transparency is a worthy goal, investors and other stakeholders in Chinese listed companies are still confronted with significant corporate governance uncertainties given state control over many enterprises, which carries the right to appoint directors, and the murky role of state-controlled financial institutions that provide significant amounts of debt financing to listed companies.

India

As opposed to other developing countries, such as China, India has a sophisticated legal system underlying its capital markets, including application of the rule of law and guaranteed property rights. Indian capital markets, including public securities exchanges such as the National Stock Exchange of India Limited (www.nseindia.com) and the Bombay Stock Exchange Limited (www.bseindia.com), have grown rapidly in recent years—they are now the world's fourth and fifth largest stock exchanges, respectively, in terms of volume of transactions although much smaller in terms of market capitalization when compared to other large exchanges around the world and have become one of the most popular global venues for initial public offerings; however, critics still complain about a lack of broad liquidity. The Indian securities regulator—the Securities and Exchange Board of India (www.sebt.gov.in)—has attempted to enforce corporate governance by imposing a rigorous regulatory regime to ensure fairness, transparency, and good practice and, in fact, is one of a growing number of securities exchange regulators that now requires that exchanges include social and/or environmental disclosure as part of their listing requirements, which means that listed companies must issue reports including social and/or environmental

---

[29] Corporate Governance of Listed Companies in China (OECD, 2011), 99–100. https://oecd.org/corporate/ca/corporategovernanceprinciples/48444985.pdf

information.[30] A number of corporate governance-related changes were made in 2014 to the Companies Act of India[31]:

- One or more women directors were recommended for certain classes of companies.
- Every company in India must have a resident directory.
- The maximum permissible directors cannot exceed 15 in a public limited company unless approved by a special resolution of the shareholders.
- Independent directors were introduced as a new concept under the Act and the Act now includes functions and duties for such directors (e.g., independent directors must attend at least one meeting a year) and a requirement for a code of conduct.
- Every company must appoint an individual or firm as an auditor and the responsibilities of the board-level audit committee have been expanded.
- Top management is required to recognize the rights of the shareholders and ensure strong co-operation between the company and its stakeholders.
- Every company has to make accurate disclosure of financial situations, performance, material matter, ownership, and governance.

Executive compensation is an issue in India, as it is in many countries; however, Indian law does require that a nomination and remuneration committee, which must have a majority of independent directors, frame

---

[30] Williams, C. 2016. "Corporate Social Responsibility and Corporate Governance." In *Oxford Handbook of Corporate Law and Governance*, eds. J. Gordon and G. Ringe, (Oxford: Oxford University Press, 2016), 16, available at http://digitalcommons.osgoode.yorku.ca/scholarly_works/1784 (citing Initiative for Responsible Investment, Corporate Social Responsibility Disclosure Efforts by National Governments and Stock Exchanges (March 12, 2015), available at http://hausercenter.org/iri/wpcontent/uploads/2011/08/CR-3-12-15.pdf).

[31] Corporate Governance in India (May 12, 2015), https://wcorpgov.net/2015/05/corporate-governance-in-india/

a policy on remuneration of key employees and that the annual remuneration paid to key executives be made public. In addition, boards of Indian companies are required to include a statement in the board's report to the shareholders indicating development and implementation of risk management policy for the company and the independent directors are mandated to assess the risk management systems of the company.[32]

In spite of all of the changes that have been made to the letter of corporate governance law in India over the last decade, real progress has been slow. For example, most companies in India tend to only comply on paper; board appointments are still by way of "word of mouth" or fellow board member recommendations and "true independence" of directors and performance evaluation of directors are still relatively new concepts within the Indian corporate governance framework. In fact, it is common for independent directors to be dismissed by promoters when the independent directors oppose actions proposed by the promoters. In addition, while changes in the law have mandated that directors owe duties not only toward the company and shareholders but also toward the employees, community, and for the protection of environment, progress has been slow and little in the way of sanctions has occurred and boards are still a long way away from full-scale engagement with stakeholders.[33]

India notably passed legislation in 2014 that required companies that had reached a certain size to establish a corporate responsibility committee at the board level and contribute at least 2 percent of their average net profits over the last three financial years to corporate responsibility initiatives.[34] The corporate responsibility committee is charged with framing a CSR policy for the company and making recommendations for spending on CSR initiatives based on the policy. If a company fails

---

[32] Unadkat, K. 2017. "Top 10 Issues in Corporate Governance Practices in India." *Association of Corporate Counsel,* http://acc.com/legalresources/publications/topten/tticgpi.cfm

[33] Id.

[34] Williams, C. 2016. "Corporate Social Responsibility and Corporate Governance." In *Oxford Handbook of Corporate Law and Governance,* eds. J. Gordon and G. Ringe, (Oxford: Oxford University Press, 2016), 13, available at http://digitalcommons.osgoode.yorku.ca/scholarly_works/1784

to meet the minimum thresholds for CSR spending the board's report must include disclosures regarding the reasons for such failure and will also likely receive a notice from India's Ministry of Corporate Affairs asking for an explanation. In some cases, the Ministry has gone further and proactively challenged companies when the Ministry felt that the reasons given were not sufficient.

Korea

The principal stock market is the Korea Exchange (www.krx.co.kr) (KRX), which was created in 2004 under the Korea Stock and Futures Exchange Act as an integration of three existing Korean spot and future exchanges. The instruments traded on the KRX include stocks, bonds, Exchange Traded Funds, Real Estate Investment Trusts, and derivatives. The principal source of securities regulation in Korea is the Financial Investment Services and Capital Market Consolidation Act (FCA). Securities regulation in Korea is carried out through the Financial Services Commission (www.fsc.go.kr). The principal means for regulating corporate governance in Korea is the Commercial Code, which is enforced by the Ministry of Justice, and there is no standalone corporate governance code in Korea. Listed companies must have a quarter or more of the board comprised of outside directors and a large-scale listed company must have three or more outside directors, and those outside directors must form the majority of the board. Unless otherwise provided for in the articles of incorporation, there are no requirements relating to the independence of directors, excluding outside directors. Korean companies are not subject to any single legal requirement or nonbinding guidance solely focused on CSR and it is not yet common for Korean companies to report on environmental, social, or ethical issues.[35]

Mexico

The Mexican Stock Exchange (Bolsa Mexicana de Valores (BMV)) (www.bmv.com.mx) is Mexico's only stock exchange and is primarily regulated

---

[35] Lee, H., and Y. Kim. 2017. *Corporate Governance and Directors' Duties in South Korea*. Thomson Reuters Practical Law.

by the Mexican Securities Market Law (SML) and circulars issued by the National Banking and Securities Commission (www.cnbv.gob.mx) (NCSB). Mexico has a Best Corporate Practices Code, which generally follows the structure and contents of the OECD Principles of Corporate Governance. Observance of the Code is currently voluntary; however, adherence to many of its principles has been made mandatory by their incorporation into the SML and listed companies in Mexico are required to annually disclose their degree of compliance with the Code. Governance practices formerly limited to listed companies and specially regulated entities, such as having independent directors and creating special board committees for audits and governance practices, are slowly being adopted by nonlisted and nonregulated entities. The lack of significant representation of women in boardrooms is being addressed by governmental initiatives to require more disclosures about the number of women on boards and implementation of gender equality policies at the board level. While CSR is not a specified legal requirement in Mexico, it is increasingly common for companies to establish CSR project policies, engage in CSR-related projects on a voluntary basis and issue annual CSR reports. It is also possible for companies to be designated as a "Socially Responsible Enterprise" by the Mexican Philanthropy Centre if they "promote a culture of responsible competitiveness that enables the success of the business while also contributing to the welfare of its community" and "reject corruption and be governed by a code of ethics, contribute to the conservation of the environment and identify and work toward the social needs of its community."[36]

Singapore

The Monetary Authority of Singapore (www.mas.gov.sg) (MAS) oversees securities regulation in Singapore, where the main exchange is the Singapore Exchange Limited (www.sgx.com) (SGX). Aspects of corporate governance for listed companies in Singapore are driven by the country's Code of Corporate Governance and the listing standards of the SGX. Key practices encouraged under the Code include having an effective board,

---

[36] Garcia-Naranjo, F. 2017. *Corporate Governance and Directors' Duties in Mexico.* Thomson Reuters Practical Law.

which is aware of its roles and responsibilities and which is provided with access to the necessary information to perform these responsibilities; having a strong independent element on the board with no concentration of power in any one person; having formal and transparent processes for board appointments, board performance, and board and executive remuneration, all of which is to be facilitated by the appointment of nomination and remuneration committees to oversee these matters; emphasizing the importance of accountability and audit and requiring the establishment of audit committees and the internal audit function; having strong internal control processes in place; and promoting greater disclosure for, and communication with, shareholders.[37]

Commentary on the country report for Singapore included in the ASEAN Corporate Governance Scorecard 2018 argued that the development of corporate governance practices in Singapore has "essentially flatlined" with a widening gap between large cap companies and the rest of the field and glaring needs for improvements in disclosure and transparency, attendance at annual general meetings and diversity practices (i.e., disclosing a detailed diversity policy and having female directors on board).[38]

The SGX has stated that "combined financial and sustainability reports enable a better assessment of the issuer's financial prospects and quality of management" and listed companies are required to publish a sustainability report under the SGX's Sustainability Reporting Guide that is based on an assessment of what the most important ESG issues are facing the business and its stakeholders and which should address the following primary components: companies should disclose what their material factors are, why they are material, and how this has been

---

[37] Yeo, V. 2018. "Corporate Governance in Singapore." ACCA, February 2018, http://accaglobal.com/us/en/student/exam-support-resources/fundamentals-exams-study-resources/f4/technical-articles/corporate-governance-singapore.html

[38] Quah, M. 2018. "Corporate Governance Progress Flatlines for Singapore Companies." *The Business Times*, April 4, 2018, https://businesstimes.com.sg/companies-markets/corporate-governance-progress-flatlines-for-singapore-companies

determined; the report should disclose the related policies, practices, and performance of the company in relation to each of the material ESG factors identified, in both descriptive and quantitative terms; the report should set out the company's targets for the forthcoming year in relation to each material ESG factor identified; the company should select a sustainability reporting framework (or frameworks) to guide its reporting and disclosure; and the report should contain a statement from the board on how ESG factors are considered as part of strategy formulation, and provide detail on its oversight of the identification, management, and monitoring of material ESG factors.

Australia

Securities regulation in Australia is the responsibility of the Australian Securities and Investments Commission (www.asic.gov.au) (ASIC) and the Australian Securities Exchange (www.asx.com.au) (ASX) is one of a growing number of stock exchanges that now requires social and/or environmental disclosure as part of its listing requirements.[39] Australia is one of the countries that require pension funds to disclose the extent to which the fund incorporates social and environmental information into its investment decisions.[40] The ASIC has issued extensive guidance on corporate governance and the specific duties and responsibilities of corporate

---

[39] Williams, C. 2016. "Corporate Social Responsibility and Corporate Governance." In *Oxford Handbook of Corporate Law and Governance*, eds. J. Gordon and G. Ringe, 16. Oxford: Oxford University Press, Available at http://digitalcommons.osgoode.yorku.ca/scholarly_works/1784 (citing Initiative for Responsible Investment, Corporate Social Responsibility Disclosure Efforts by National Governments and Stock Exchanges (March 12, 2015), available at http://hausercenter.org/iri/wpcontent/uploads/2011/08/CR-3-12-15.pdf).

[40] Williams, C. 2016. "Corporate Social Responsibility and Corporate Governance." In *Oxford Handbook of Corporate Law and Governance*, eds. J. Gordon and G. Ringe, 16. Oxford: Oxford University Press. Available at http://digitalcommons.osgoode.yorku.ca/scholarly_works/1784 (citing Initiative for Responsible Investment, Corporate Social Responsibility Disclosure Efforts by National Governments and Stock Exchanges (March 12, 2015), available at http://hausercenter.org/iri/wpcontent/uploads/2011/08/CR-3-12-15.pdf).

directors.[41] Sustainability reporting has improved significantly among the largest companies on the ASX according to annual assessments issued by Australian Council of Superannuation Investors (www.acsi.org.au).

Canada

Securities regulation in Canada is overseen by the Canadian Securities Administrators (www.csa-acvm.ca) (CSA) and the largest securities exchange in Canada is the Toronto Stock Exchange and TSX Venture Exchange (www.tmx.com). Canada is one of the countries that require pension funds to disclose the extent to which the fund incorporates social and environmental information into its investment decisions.[42] Canada's system of corporate governance has been aptly described as follows:

> Canada's system of corporate governance is derived from the British common law model and strongly influenced by developments in the United States. While corporate governance practices in the United Kingdom and the United States are similar in many respects, where there are differences Canadian practice usually falls somewhere in between. For example, a Canadian corporation is more likely than a US corporation to have a chair who is not the CEO, and typically has fewer executives on the board than a UK corporation.[43]

As in the United States, Canadian corporations must contend with regulation of corporate and securities matters at both the federal and

---

[41] https://asic.gov.au/regulatory-resources/corporate-governance/

[42] Williams, C. 2016. "Corporate Social Responsibility and Corporate Governance." In *Oxford Handbook of Corporate Law and Governance*, eds. 16. Oxford: Oxford University Press, available at http://digitalcommons.osgoode.yorku.ca/scholarly_works/1784 (citing Initiative for Responsible Investment, Corporate Social Responsibility Disclosure Efforts by National Governments and Stock Exchanges (March 12, 2015), Available at http://hausercenter.org/iri/wpcontent/uploads/2011/08/CR-3-12-15.pdf).

[43] MacDougall, A., R. Yalden, and J. Valley. "Canada." In *The Corporate Governance Review*, ed. W. Calkoen, 7 ed., 72.

provincial levels; however, the federal government and the provinces are continuously collaborating on developing and maintaining a cooperative and consistent governance framework. Also relevant are legal rules and best practices promoted by institutional shareholder groups, the media and professional director associations such as the Institute of Corporate Directors.[44] Dominant and emerging issues in corporate governance in recent years have included shareholder engagement and activism; diversity in corporate leadership positions and board renewal; takeover bids and defensive tactics; proxy adviser initiatives; and risk management.[45] Like in the United States, corporate governance practices regarding ESG matters in Canada have been the focus of regulators and members of the investment community and the role of corporate directors in the area will be substantially impacted by the interpretation of the directors' duty of loyalty by the Supreme Court of Canada to require consideration of a wide range of stakeholders and a broadening range of risks. It is expected that in the near future updated guidance will be released by the CSA calling for enhanced disclosures of risks relating to climate change and more regulatory focus on cyber security is expected.[46]

---

[44] Id.

[45] Andreone, R., and C. Ortved. May 2018. *Corporate Governance and Directors' Duties in Canada*. Thomson Reuters Practical Law.

[46] Id.

CHAPTER 6

CSR-Related Nonprofits and NGOs

During the first years after corporate social responsibility (CSR) began to emerge as an issue for businesses in the 1980s, it was largely a self-regulated activity, with companies making their own decisions about how to manage and report on their environmental and social performance. While the achievements of some firms were impressive, overall there was skepticism about the honesty of corporate communications on their non-economic performance and many argued that corporate self-regulation was inadequate and that it made it too easy for firms to simply engage in public relations activities to improve their reputations as opposed to making a meaningful contribution to sustainable development and achieving social responsibility. One of the responses to these concerns was the ascendance of a new model of coregulation, which now includes partnerships of various types between companies and nonprofit organizations. In addition, nonprofit organizations have become important direct actors with respect to organizing and undertaking CSR-related initiatives.

Nonprofits

Nonprofit organizations are legal entities formed by a group of person to promote cultural, religious, professional, or social objectives. Each jurisdiction has its own legal definition of a nonprofit and in the United States the key characteristics include organization for purposes other than generating a profit and prohibitions on any part of the organization's income being distributed to its members, directors, or officers. Nonprofit status is based on pursuit of certain types of purposes including religious, charitable, scientific, public safety, literary, or educational. Nonprofits include charities, membership groups formed around a common interest in a subject or activity (e.g., sports), social or recreational organizations, public education institutions, public hospitals, public arts organizations, and trade unions.

In the United States, the predominant form of nonprofit organization is the corporation. There are several distinctions between nonprofit and profit corporations: a business corporation generally exists to make a profit for its shareholders; however, a nonprofit corporation (particularly a charitable organization) exists primarily to advance a purpose or objective; a business corporation ultimately benefits the shareholder or shareholders, but nonprofit corporations generally do not have shareholders and are not even required to have a class of members that the organization serves (however, in many cases a corporate foundation will be organized as a nonprofit corporation with a single member, the company that is sponsoring the foundation, so that the sponsor can exert influence over the corporation's activities); the goal and focus of the management of charitable organizations should be to advance the entity's stated purposes, rather than the interests of any group of individuals affiliated with the charity; and although nonprofit organizations need revenues to sustain their operations, much of these revenues will be in the form of contributions or grants (i.e., contributions from the company in the case of a corporate foundation); the pursuit of enterprises or activities solely to generate a profit can jeopardize an organization's tax-exempt status.

For most nonprofit corporations, including all charitable organizations, if the organization desires preferential tax treatment, it must apply to the state taxing authority for a determination of the entity's exempt status. In addition, nonprofit corporations must also apply to the Internal Revenue Service (IRS) for a determination of exempt status for federal income tax purposes, unless the organization qualifies for an exception to this requirement, as in the case of religious organizations having an annual income of less than $5,000. Exempt organizations are initially divided between public charities and private foundations, each of which are required to file annual information returns with the IRS but are subject to very different tax rules that have important consequences on how the organization is operated. Public charities are, as the name implies, publicly supported and include organizations like the United Way and March of Dimes, as well as churches, schools, and hospitals, and received

favored treatment under the IRC. While companies launching and sponsoring corporate foundations usually expect to underwrite the activities
on their own it is possible for such a foundation to raise a significant
amount of funds through fundraising and qualify as a public charity if at
least one third of its support comes from the general public. In contrast,
private foundations are not publicly supported and are divided between
operating foundations and nonoperating foundations. Many companies
prefer private foundation status because it is consistent with the reten-
tion of control over the mission of the corporate foundation and the
use of the funds contributed by the company. A private foundation may
be controlled by a single donor or a small group of donors need not be
concerned with fundraising from outsiders in order to satisfy the public
support test imposed on public charities. However, a private foundation
must adhere to certain operational restrictions in order to maintain tax
exempt status and avoid excise taxes and other penalties.[1]

Nonprofit corporations are formed pursuant to state statutes and each
state has its own specific requirements with respect to the formation and
organization of nonprofit corporations (many states will require that corporate foundations be formed as a "public benefit corporation," one of
several types of nonprofit corporations recognized by statute). As with
for-profit corporations, each nonprofit corporation must have a board of
directors. Many nonprofit corporations, particularly larger organizations
engaged in substantial fundraising activities, are implementing corporate governance schemes similar to those found in the private sector. For
example, a nonprofit corporation may establish an audit committee to
oversee the financial reporting system established and maintained by the

---

[1] Among other things, a private foundation must: satisfy minimum annual
payout requirements of at least 5 percent of the fair market value of the previous year's assets; pay a 2 percent tax annually on net investment income; avoid
self-dealing transactions with insiders; limit its ownership interest in any one
business to 20 percent in order to avoid "excess business holdings"; avoid risky
investments that jeopardize the accomplishment of the foundation's charitable
purposes, which means that the foundation will need to perform rigorous due
diligence before making an investment; and avoid contributions to individuals, other private foundations or non-charitable organizations, which might be
deemed to be "taxable expenditures."

corporation and should promulgate a statement of purpose and objectives for the committee. In fact, some states have actually begun requiring nonprofit corporations of a certain size engaging in charitable activities to have an audit committee. Another common governance tool is an executive compensation committee that will oversee compensation for the executive director and other senior managerial staff of the corporation. Once again, it is useful for the board of directors to adopt guidelines for the deliberations of the executive compensation committee. Depending on the situation, the board of directors may also establish governance, nominating and finance committees, particularly when the nonprofit begins to grow and its constituencies demand transparency with respect to the composition of the board, solicitation, and use of funds and good governance practices such as conflict-of-interest policies and procedures.

The growing trend in many states is to require nonprofit corporations and other unincorporated associations to prepare annual reports signed by directors and senior officers of the organization that provide information on fundraising activities, uses of funds, governance procedures, compensation, and transactions entered into by the association that might raise concerns about conflicts of interest. In addition, directors and other leaders of nonprofit organizations should consider and implement recognized best practices for governance that include an active, independent, and qualified governing board supported by adequate resources and training; a competent and engaged CEO/executive director; governing board processes; a clear organizational mission formalized in a written mission statement; a strategic planning and budgeting process; processes for regulatory compliance and risk management, especially with respect to fund-raising activities; human resources management processes; community relations processes; and processes relating to disclosure and reporting, conflicts of interest and recordkeeping.

Various states have special registration requirements that might apply to various types of nonprofit corporations. For example, California's Uniform Supervision of Trustees for Charitable Purposes Act (California Act) imposes various filing, registration, and reporting requirements on charitable corporations (other than religious corporations), unincorporated associations, trustees, and other legal entities holding property for charitable purposes. Nonprofit corporations are also required to keep the following as permanent records: minutes of all meetings of its members and board of directors; a record of all actions taken by the members or directors without a meeting; and a record of all actions taken by committees of the board of directors. In addition, the corporation must maintain appropriate accounting records[2] and the corporation or its agent must maintain a record of its members in a form that permits preparation of a list of the name and address of all members, in alphabetical order by class, showing the number of votes each member is entitled to cast. Finally, the following records must be kept by a nonprofit corporation at its principal office: charters documents; certain board resolutions and directors' meeting minutes; written communications with members; a list of the names and business addresses of directors and officers; and its most recent annual report delivered to the secretary of state.[2]

NGOs

Nongovernmental organizations, which are often referred to as "NGOs," emerged in 1945 with the creation of the United Nations and have been described as nonprofit making associations formed by the citizens who are not part of the government and that function completely autonomously from the government to perform a broad spectrum of services and humanitarian functions, draw attention of governments and businesses to specific issues and grievances, advocate public policies, and promote political participation by providing information. NGOs are actually an important subset of the broader sector of nonprofit organizations, distinguishable largely by their national and international efforts as opposed to the narrower local focus of smaller nonprofits.[3] In fact, NGO is not a regulated term in the United States and U.S.-based groups engaged in the activities typically associated with an NGO will comply with the requirements for recognition as a nonprofit organization. The term NGO

---

[2] For further discussion of formation and organization of nonprofit corporations, and maintenance of nonprofit status for tax purposes, see Gutterman, A. 2020. *Community Engagement and Investment.* New York: Business Expert Press.
[3] NGOs have been defined as "formal (professional) independent societal organizations whose primary aim is to promote common goals at the national or the international level." See Martens, K. 2002. "Mission impossible? Defining Nongovernmental Organizations." *Voluntas: Journal of Voluntary and Nonprofit Organizations* 13, no. 3, p. 271.

is generally used for groups that come together and are managed outside of the United States and such groups must register with the governments of the jurisdictions in which they operate in order to obtain NGO status.[4]

NGOs typically gather financial and other support from governments, foundations, businesses, and private groups and individuals and frequently operate worldwide with activities and supporters in a number of countries. NGOs are also known as "civil society" and various types of NGOs have been identified such as donor organized NGOs, environmental NGOs, technical assistance NGOs, grassroots support organizations, and market advocacy organizations. NGOs generally focus their efforts on specific issues such as supporting human rights, women and children's rights, environmental or health issues, community development, and setting standards. A representative list of the duties that might be carried out by an NGO includes:

- Community health promotion and education (such as hygiene and waste disposal).
- Managing emerging health crises (HIV/AIDS, Hepatitis B).
- Community social problems (juvenile crimes, run-aways, street children, prostitution)
- Environmental (sustainable water and energy resources)
- Economic (micro loans, skills training, financial education, and consulting)
- Development (school and infrastructure construction)
- Women's issues (women's and children's rights, counseling, literacy issues).

---

[4] The discussion of NGOs in this section is adapted from various sources including Differences between NGO and NPO (July 29, 2017), https://keydifferences. com/difference-between-ngo-and-npo.html; and Key Differences between Non-Government Organizations (NGO) and Non-Profit Organizations (NPO), https://cmu.edu/career/documents/industry-guides/NGOs%20and%20NPOs. pdf; and Differences Between NGOs and Nonprofits, https://thebalancesmb. com/differences-between-ngos-and-nonprofits-4589762 Among the sources for additional information on NGOs is the website of InterAction (https:// interaction.org/), which is a Washington, DC, alliance of almost 200 US-based international NGOs.

Well-known U.S.-based NGOs, which also operate across borders, include the American Red Cross, Salvation Army, Greenpeace, PETA, and the American Civil Liberties Union. As for NGOs headquartered outside of the United States, but having significant contacts with supporters in the United States, notice should be taken of the International Olympic Committee, Amnesty International, and the International AIDS Society.

A subset of NGOs sometimes referred to as "social purpose NGOs" have played the biggest roles in the CSR arena and include a range of environmental groups, human rights organizations, and organizations dedicated to addressing and alleviating serious sustainable development problems such as poverty. The number and breadth of operations of these NGOs has been continuously expanded and has been accelerated and supported by an overall feeling among consumers and members of civil society that NGOs are trustworthy and reliable. A number of NGOs have developed their own valuable brands, making them some of the best-known organizations in the world: Amnesty International, Greenpeace, Oxfam, Save the Children, and the World Wildlife Fund (WWF). Moreover, as NGOs have become more prevalent, the creativity and complexity of their relationships with businesses has also matured. In 2014, for example, Poret called out partnerships between Coca-Cola Company and WWF to help protect the world's seven most important fresh water river basins, Chiquita Brand, and the Rainforest Alliance to cultivate bananas in a more environmentally friendly manner and McDonalds and the Environmental Defense Fund to reduce the environmental impact of McDonalds' packaging. Another significant contribution of NGOs has come through their roles as standards setters or certifying agencies in a number of fields including sustainable agriculture, fishing, packaging, supply chain management, labor issues, renewable energy, forest resources, health, and safety, an important role given that voluntary certification and eco-labeling have become important elements of CSR strategies for businesses of all sizes.[5]

When NGOs first emerged, many of the interactions between and businesses could be characterized as "confrontational," such as when

---

[5] Poret, S. 2014. *Corporate-HGO Partnerships in CSR Activities: Why and How?*, 2–3. Paris: Ecole Polytechnique Department of Economics.

NGOs supported and organized boycotts of companies based on per-ceived shortcomings in their environmental or social practices. As a result, businesses were initially leery of working with NGOs; however, as time has gone by collaboration has become the norm and businesses have become more comfortable working with NGOs and see them as valuable partners in overcoming barriers to acceptance and expansion of CSR.[6] Poret argued that the emergence of NGOs can be attributed in part to their ability to contribute to solutions of market failures. As mentioned previously, early CSR efforts were widely criticized on the basis that firms were simply setting their own rules and there was no way to verify claims regarding environmental and social performance. NGOs intervened into the information gap by providing consumers and other stakeholders with an independent source of data that could be used in purchasing decisions. As time has gone by, businesses know and understand that in order for them to credibly promote a product or service as sustainable they must be willing and able to offer a "warranty" in the form of adherence to certifi-cation and labeling systems and standards typically overseen by NGOs. As explained by Poret, "NGOs act as certifying agencies that assure consumers that the products that they have purchased were produced in a sustainable manner . . . [thus] allow[ing] firms to credibly signal that their products possess sustainable attributes."[7]

For their part, NGOs began to see that moving away from constant confrontation with businesses toward a more collaborative relationship that could have long-term benefits for them as well. Obviously, being able to work with a large company allows an NGO to expand its reach beyond what it could do on its own and thus generate greater impact in the envi-ronmental and social areas of interest to it. Collaboration also allows an NGO to increase its own notoriety as word spreads that it is working with a well-known brand, thus strengthen the NGOs credibility, reputation, and political influence. In addition, of course, partnering with for-profit

---

[6] Id. at 3 (citing Kourula, A., and S. Laasonen. 2010. "Nongovernmental Organizations in Business and Society, Management, and International Business Research—Review and Implications from 1998 to 2007." *Business and Society* 49, no. 1, p. 68.

[7] Id. at 11–12.

businesses provides NGOs with sources of funding, no small matter given that public funding for the activities typically conducted by NGOs has declined precipitously and competition for capital has increased as the number of NGOs has expanded and fund-raising efforts have become more sophisticated. While it is apparent that NGOs can benefit from corporate partnering, they nonetheless must be mindful of various risks that if left unattended can ultimately undercut their overall mission. For example, NGOs must choose their corporate partners carefully, since a scandal relating to a partner will almost certainly have an adverse impact on the reputation of the NGO. NGOs must also maintain their independence and resist the urge to compromise in their standards in order to secure the agreement of a particular firm to implement them.[8]

Companies need to realize that NGOs can play a wide range of roles in their CSR programs and initiatives and that the path toward integrating NGOs into their CSR strategy begins with identifying the best and most valuable fit. Poret explained that companies have partnered with NGOs because NGOs promote societal actions that the company wishes to support, provide technical assistance, elaborate and administer certification schemes, promote and design CSR standards and management, and reporting processes and participate in CSR monitoring and auditing.[9] Common approaches that companies might consider to involve NGOs in their sustainability programs, each of which is distinguished by different levels of involvement and collaboration between the parties, include[10]:

- Companies may enter into a cobranding arrangement with an NGO that can be used to communicate their commitment to a cause or issue associated with the activities of the NGO. For example, WWF has established a well-known cobranding program with its Panda logo that has been joined by companies promoting a wide range of products and services who are interested in projecting an environmentally

---

[8] Id. at 12–13.
[9] Id. at 15–16.
[10] Id. at 14–15.

friendly image and strengthening trust and loyalty among consumers. Eligibility depends on the products meeting environmental and social criteria established by WWF and products must pass independent certification through labeling or certification schemes approved by WWF.

- One of the basic and most commonly used internal instruments of CSR is a code of conduct approved by the board of directors and applicable to officers, employees, contractors, and business partners. NGOs are often involved in the drafting of model codes that companies can adopt "as is" or with minor variances to account for specific circumstances. In those cases, companies may contract with the NGO to act as an independent and knowledgeable monitoring agency of the implementation of the code and the NGO will perform independent compliance audits of all elements of the code.

- In situations where there is no widely recognized code of conduct covering a particular product or activities, a company may form an alliance with an NGO (and other companies) to develop a new code of conduct or a specific standard along with evaluation mechanisms with independent enforcement or certification by parties that have been formally vetted by the NGO as the recognized accreditation body. Obviously this is a challenging and time-consuming undertaking; however, companies may choose this route as a way to both improve their performance in terms of quality and sustainability and establish themselves as innovators in the field.

- Companies may seek the advantages of associating with a well-regarded NGO by conforming their products to the criteria necessary to qualify for certifications or labels owned by the NGO. As opposed to the dialogue inherent in developing a code of conduct in collaboration with an NGO, certification and labeling requires that companies must understand and fully comply with standards that have been established by the NGO in advance and companies must weigh the costs of changes in product characteristics (e.g., design, ingredients, packaging, etc.) against the benefits of public association with the NGO.

Writing in the late 1980s, Drucker referred to NGOs as the "third sector" (the first two being private and public or government) that would increasingly play a very valuable role for both firms and society, and Giovannucci et al. explained that while NGOs have relatively little economic power they do have a unique value proposition: social credibility among consumers and media that businesses seek to tap into via partnerships in order to enhance their own social legitimacy.[11] Voluntary standards are among the partnerships that NGOs have been involved with and through those activities NGOs have contributed to the development of a normative framework, assured by independent certification, which corporations can use for social legitimacy.[12] For their part, businesses welcome the participation of NGOs in the development of voluntary standards because the publicly generally trusts the motives of NGOs and their ability to provide effective management and oversight to the standards initiatives.[13]

Social Responsibility Organizations

By definition, many nonprofits, particularly those formed as public benefit corporations, are formed for public or charitable purposes and advancing a purpose or objective related thereto, as opposed to making a profit for shareholders or otherwise furthering the interests of any group of individuals affiliated with the entity. In this chapter, an effort has been made to distinguish nonprofits and NGOs that are primarily focused on environmental or human rights issues; however, many nonprofits and

---

[11] Giovannucci, D., O. von Hagen, and J. Wozniak. 2014. "Corporate Social Responsibility and the Role of Voluntary Sustainability Standards." In *Voluntary Standards Systems*, eds. C. Schmitz-Hoffmann et al. 359–366, Berlin: Springer-Verlag. (citing Drucker, P. 1989. "What Business can Learn from Nonprofits." *Harvard Business Review* 67, no. 4, p. 88.

[12] Id. (citing Giovannucci, D., and S. Ponte. 2005. "Standards as a New Form of Social Contract?: Sustainability Initiatives in the Coffee Industry." *Food Policy* 30, no. 3, p. 284).

[13] For further discussion of NGOs, including considerations for partnering with NGOs to pursue sustainability initiatives, see Gutterman, A. 2019. *Sustainability Governance and Management: A Guide for Sustainable Entrepreneurs.* Oakland CA: Sustainable Entrepreneurship Project.

NGOs engage in activities that address other important social responsibility issues such as business development, communities, compliance, employees, governance, operations, products and services, supply chain management, and transportation and logistics and provide various types of support including capital, technology, research, and training.

The Academy of Business in Society

The Academy of Business in Society (ABIS) (https://abis-global.org/about/) is a global network of over 100 companies and academic institutions whose expertise, commitment, and resources are leveraged to invest in a more sustainable future for business in society through research and education. ABIS (formerly known as EABIS, the European Academy of Business in Society) was founded in 2001 and launched at INSEAD in 2002 with the support of the leading business schools in Europe in partnership with IBM, Microsoft, Johnson & Johnson, Unilever, and Shell. Since it was launched ABIS has delivered 90+ knowledge development and learning initiatives; secured a significant amount of EU grants to fund CSR research projects; and participated in the creation of the UN Global Compact Principles for Responsible Management Education.

African Institute of Corporate Citizenship

The African Institute of Corporate Citizenship (AICC) (www.aiccafrica.org) is a nongovernmental organization established in 2001 in South Africa with a main mandate is to promote the role of business in development. AICC has operated on a partnership model and has been involved in projects with partner organizations in a number of countries in Africa including South Africa, Malawi, Botswana, Lesotho, Mozambique, Namibia, Nigeria, Zambia, and Zimbabwe. AICC is committed to being the center of excellence in corporate citizenship in Africa and it focuses on the role of business in building sustainable communities. One of AICC's broad objectives it to achieve responsible growth and competitiveness throughout Africa by ensuring that enterprises, as good citizens, change the way they do business in a way which benefits people, the economy, and the environment. Stated core values of AICC and its stakeholders include integrity, hard work, diligence, wisdom, impartiality, and team spirit.

Business Roundtable

The Business Roundtable (www.businessroundtable.org/about-us) is a nonprofit association based in Washington, DC, whose members are chief executive officers (CEOs) of major U.S. companies with more than 15 million employees and more than $7 trillion in annual revenues as of 2019. The Business Roundtable has periodically issued Principles of Corporate Governance since 1978. On August 19, 2019, the Business Roundtable announced the release of an updated Statement on the Purpose of a Corporation signed by 181 CEOs that redefined the purpose of a corporation as stated in previous principles to move away from shareholder primacy (i.e., that corporations exist principally to serve shareholders, a concept that had been championed in the principles since 1997) to promotion of an economy that serves all Americans and included commitments to operate companies for the benefit of all stakeholders: customers, employees, suppliers, communities, and shareholders. Several of the CEOs explained that the changes were necessary in order to reflect the way that companies can and should operate and the essential role that companies must be willing to play in improving society through job creation, innovation, and delivery of crucial goods and services. The updated principles also explicitly recognized that CEOs needed to look beyond generating profits and returning value only to shareholders to building long-term value for all stakeholders.

The Statement on the Purpose of a Corporation reads as follows:

> Americans deserve an economy that allows each person to succeed through hard work and creativity and to lead a life of meaning and dignity. We believe the free-market system is the best means of generating good jobs, a strong and sustainable economy, innovation, a healthy environment and economic opportunity for all.
>
> Businesses play a vital role in the economy by creating jobs, fostering innovation and providing essential goods and services. Businesses make and sell consumer products; manufacture

equipment and vehicles; support the national defense; grow and produce food; provide health care; generate and deliver energy; and offer financial, communications and other services that underpin economic growth.

While each of our individual companies serves its own corporate purpose, we share a fundamental commitment to all of our stakeholders. We commit to:

- Delivering value to our customers. We will further the tradition of American companies leading the way in meeting or exceeding customer expectations.
- Investing in our employees. This starts with compensating them fairly and providing important benefits. It also includes supporting them through training and education that help develop new skills for a rapidly changing world. We foster diversity and inclusion, dignity and respect.
- Dealing fairly and ethically with our suppliers. We are dedicated to serving as good partners to the other companies, large and small, that help us meet our missions.
- Supporting the communities in which we work. We respect the people in our communities and protect the environment by embracing sustainable practices across our businesses.
- Generating long-term value for shareholders, who provide the capital that allows companies to invest, grow and innovate. We are committed to transparency and effective engagement with shareholders.

Each of our stakeholders is essential. We commit to deliver value to all of them, for the future success of our companies, our communities and our country.

Business Social Compliance Initiative

The Business Social Compliance Initiative, now Amfori BSCI (www. amfori.org/content/amfori-bsci), was created in 2003 by the Foreign

Trade Association to provide companies with a practical and efficient system to improve social compliance within the factories and farms in their global supply chains. The BSCI refers to itself as the leading global business association for open and sustainable trade, bringing together over 2,400 retailers, importers, brands, and associations from more than 40 countries with a combined turnover of more than one trillion euros as of 2019. The BSCI has promulgated a common code of conduct with 11 principles designed to improve social performance in supply chains that are based on the principal international labor standards protecting workers' rights such as International Labor Organization (ILO) conventions and declarations, the United Nations Guiding Principles on Business and Human Rights and guidelines for multinational enterprises of the Organization for Economic Co-operation and Development.[14] The BSCI also provides support for the implementation of its code of conduct through a broad range of tools and activities to audit, train, share information, and influence key actors toward improving labor conditions in the supply chain of participating companies. The BSCI makes it clear that it is not an auditing company, accreditation system, or certificate scheme; however, it does provide a network of external accredited, experienced, and independent auditing companies that conduct social audits based on the BSCI approach.

Business for Social Responsibility

Business for Social Responsibility (BSR) is a global nonprofit organization (www.bsr.org) that works with its network of more than 250 member companies and other partners to build a just and sustainable world. From its offices in Asia, Europe, and North America, BSR develops sustainable business strategies and solutions through consulting, research, and

---

[14] BSCI argued that a single code of conduct was valuable and useful given that many companies and associations, attempting to cope with inadequate or poorly enforced laws in a number of different countries at the same time, had been forced to try and create their own individual codes of conduct and implementation systems, resulting in confusion and unnecessary duplication of efforts and costs for retailers, importers and brands as well as their producers.

cross-sector collaboration. BSR teams focus on six core areas including climate change, human rights, inclusive economy, supply chain sustainability, sustainability management, and women's empowerment, and also have deep experience in a number of specific industry sectors. BSR releases information through a variety of channels including case studies, reports, primers, and conferences.

Business in the Community

Business in the Community: The Prince's Responsible Business Network (www.bitc.org.uk) claims to be the oldest and largest business-led membership organization dedicated to responsible business, having been created during the 1970s by The Prince of Wales to champion responsible business. The organization is dedicated to inspiring, engaging, and challenging its members to create a skilled, inclusive workforce today and for the future, build thriving communities in which to live and work, and innovate to repair and sustain our planet. The organizational membership includes hundreds of businesses, large and small, who can participate in programs and campaigns relating to leadership, environment and sustainability, employment and diversity, education, and communities.

Caux Round Table Principles for Business

One of the most interesting stakeholder-focused standards for corporate governance has been developed by the Caux Round Table (CRT) (www.cauxroundtable.org), which describes itself as an international network of principled business leaders working to promote a moral capitalism. The CRT believes that the world business community should play an important role in improving economic and social conditions and, to that end, has developed the CRT Principles for Business to embody the aspiration of principled business leadership. The CRT has been proactively advocating implementation of the CRT Principles at the firm level and has created a specially designed process for incorporating the CRT Principles into the culture of a corporation and is also working on ethical training for corporate boards of directors and a new ethics curriculum for business schools. The CRT Principles are rooted in two basic ethical ideals: the Japanese concept of "*kyosei*," which means living and working together for the common good enabling cooperation and mutual prosperity to coexist with healthy and fair competition; and the "human dignity," which is described in the Introduction to the CRT Principles as referring to the sacredness or value of each person as an end, not simply as a means to the fulfillment of others' purposes or even majority prescription.

The Preamble to the CRT Principles acknowledges that the mobility of employment, capital, products, and technology is making business increasingly global in its transactions and its effects and argues that law and market forces are necessary but insufficient guides for conduct. Noting that businesses can be powerful agents of positive social change, the CRT Principals admonish businesses that they are expected to act responsibly and demonstrate respect for the dignity and interest of its stakeholders (i.e., customers, employees, owners/investors, suppliers, competitors, and communities) in the policies and actions. The following General Principles in the CRT Principles were intended to serve as a foundation for dialogue and action by business leaders in search of business responsibility and a means implementing moral values into business decision making:

- Principle 1. The responsibilities of businesses extend beyond shareholders toward stakeholders
- Principle 2. The economic and social impact of business should be focused on innovation, justice, and world community
- Principle 3. Business behavior should extend beyond the letter of the law toward a spirit of trust
- Principle 4. Respect for rules
- Principle 5. Support for multilateral trade
- Principle 6. Respect for the environment
- Principle 7. Avoidance of illicit operations

Of particular interest are the various Stakeholder Principles in Section 3 of the CRT Principles:

Customers: We believe in treating all customers with dignity, irrespective of whether they purchase our products and services directly from us or otherwise acquire them in the market. We therefore have a responsibility to:

- Provide our customers with the highest quality products and services consistent with their requirements;
- Treat our customers fairly in all aspects of our business transactions, including a high level of service and remedies for their dissatisfaction;
- Make every effort to ensure that the health and safety of our customers, as well as the quality of their environment, will be sustained or enhanced by our products and services;
- Assure respect for human dignity in products offered, marketing, and advertising; and Respect the integrity of the culture of our customers.

Employees: We believe in the dignity of every employee and in taking employee interests seriously. We therefore have a responsibility to

- Provide jobs and compensation that improve workers' living conditions;
- Provide working conditions that respect each employee's health and dignity;
- Be honest in communications with employees and open in sharing information, limited only by legal and competitive constraints;
- Listen to and, where possible, act on employee suggestions, ideas, requests, and complaints;
- Engage in good faith negotiations when conflict arises;
- Avoid discriminatory practices and guarantee equal treatment and opportunity in areas such as gender, age, race, and religion;

- Promote in the business itself the employment of differently abled people in places of work where they can be genuinely useful;
- Protect employees from avoidable injury and illness in the workplace;
- Encourage and assist employees in developing relevant and transferable skills and knowledge; and
- Be sensitive to the serious unemployment problems frequently associated with business decisions, and work with governments, employee groups, other agencies, and each other in addressing these dislocations.

Owners/Investors: We believe in honoring the trust our investors place in us. We therefore have a responsibility to

- Apply professional and diligent management in order to secure a fair and competitive return on our owners' investment;
- Disclose relevant information to owners/investors subject to legal requirements and competitive constraints;
- Conserve, protect, and increase the owners/investors' assets; and
- Respect owners/investors' requests, suggestions, complaints, and formal resolutions.

Suppliers: Our relationship with suppliers and subcontractors must be based on mutual respect. We therefore have a responsibility to

- Seek fairness and truthfulness in all our activities, including pricing, licensing, and rights to sell;
- Ensure that our business activities are free from coercion and unnecessary litigation;
- Foster long-term stability in the supplier relationship in return for value, quality, competitiveness, and reliability;
- Share information with suppliers and integrate them into our planning processes;

- Pay suppliers on time and in accordance with agreed terms of trade; and
- Seek, encourage, and prefer suppliers and subcontractors whose employment practices respect human dignity.

Competitors: We believe that fair economic competition is one of the basic requirements for increasing the wealth of nations and ultimately for making possible the just distribution of goods and services. We therefore have a responsibility to

- Foster open markets for trade and investment;
- Promote competitive behavior that is socially and environmentally beneficial and demonstrates mutual respect among competitors;
- Refrain from either seeking or participating in questionable payments or favors to secure competitive advantages;
- Respect both tangible and intellectual property rights; and
- Refuse to acquire commercial information by dishonest or unethical means, such as industrial espionage.

Communities: We believe that as global corporate citizens we can contribute to such forces of reform and human rights as are at work in the communities in which we operate. We therefore have a responsibility in those communities to

- Respect human rights and democratic institutions, and promote them wherever practicable;
- Recognize government's legitimate obligation to the society at large and support public policies and practices that promote human development through harmonious relations between business and other segments of society;
- Collaborate with those forces in the community dedicated to raising standards of health, education, workplace safety and economic well-being;
- Promote and stimulate sustainable development and play a leading role in preserving and enhancing the physical environment and conserving the earth's resources;

- Support peace, security, diversity, and social integration;
- Respect the integrity of local cultures; and
- Be a good corporate citizen through charitable donations, educational and cultural contributions, and employee participation in community and civic affairs.

Ceres

Ceres, a nonprofit organization advocating for sustainability leadership (www.ceres.org), has developed and disseminated its Ceres Roadmap as a resource to help companies reengineer themselves to confront and overcome environmental and social challenges and as a guide toward corporate sustainability leadership.[15] The roadmap was first released in 2010 and has been subsequently revised to take into account rapidly emerging changes such as the following:

- Businesses had come to realize that ecological and social threats were becoming an increasingly bigger part of the environments in which they are operating and that they must be better prepared to confront climate change and a global water crisis.
- The international community, often under the auspices of global organizations such as the United Nations, had come together to develop sustainable development goals and negotiate multinational agreements on important environmental and social issues such as reducing carbon emissions and reliance on fossil fuels and providing decent work and economic growth for all segments of the population.
- The roles and responsibilities of companies to protect human rights had been defined in instruments such as the Guiding Principles on Business and Human Rights and guidance for companies on how to report on human rights had become widely available.
- Interest in sustainable companies was increasing among investors and data indicated substantial increases in the use of

---

[15] Ceres, The Ceres Roadmap for Sustainability (www.ceres.org/ceresroadmap).

environmental, social, and governance (ESG) metrics among mutual fund managers.

- Promising, albeit incremental, improvements were being made with respect to how companies were integrating sustainability into their decision-making processes, particularly in areas such as board oversight of material sustainability issues, proactive corporate engagement of investors on ESG risks and opportunities, and heightened focus on the environmental and social performance of their suppliers.

- Companies have become more and more aware of the opportunities associated with engaging and overcoming sustainability challenges included improving competitiveness, achieving savings through energy productivity initiatives, accessing and retaining top talent, strengthening values chains and realizing benefits from investments in clean technology and energy.

The revision of the Roadmap (see www.ceres.org/roadmap) announced during the mid-point of the 2010s laid out 20 expectations in the areas of governance for sustainability, stakeholder engagement, disclosure, and performance that Ceres believed that companies should seek to meet by 2020 in order to transform into truly sustainable enterprises. The first three areas fell under the general principle of "accountability," which Ceres explained as follows: "In order to realize meaningful and long-lasting sustainability performance improvements, companies must institute accountability mechanisms that integrate sustainability considerations into core business systems and decision making." Ceres noted that the expectations in those areas are focused on companies establishing and formalizing accountability for sustainability across the entire enterprise. As for performance, Ceres explained that it was "about achieving on-the-ground results, reducing carbon emissions, conserving water and other natural resources, protecting human rights, building a supply chain that meets high environmental and social standards, designing products that not only minimize sustainability impacts throughout their lifecycle, but also serve as solutions to key sustainability challenges, and proactively engaging a diverse workforce." The performance-related expectations, which were expressed as five "visions" (i.e., operations, supply chain, transportation and logistics, products and services, and employees) and accompanied by two or more guidelines for achieving those visions, focused on building systems across the company's value chain to enable ongoing performance improvements in three priority environmental and social impact areas including climate change, natural resources, and human rights.[16]

Conference Board

The Conference Board, Inc. (TCB) (www.conference-board.org) is a nonprofit global, independent business membership and research association working in the public interest to provide the world's leading organizations with the practical knowledge they need to improve their performance and better serve society. Founded over 100 years ago, TCB, which has offices in the United States, Europe, and Asia, is organized around centers focusing on economic development/public policy; economy, strategy, and finance; environmental, social, and governance (ESG); human capital and marketing and communications, each of which support a portfolio of councils that allow leaders from TCB members to meet and collaborate to address specific topics and issues. With respect to ESG, the focus is on corporate governance, sustainability, and corporate citizenship and philanthropy and working groups address specific issues such as integrated reporting, corporate political spending, and cybersecurity. Members can take advantage of the TCB's Sustainability Practice Dashboard; tools for public companies to stay abreast of shareholder activism, track AGM votes, and compare takeover defenses against peer groups; and the TCB ESG Center, which offers a portfolio of data and analyses on corporate governance, proxy voting, sustainability, citizenship,

---

[16] For further discussion of the specific expectations in the Ceres Roadmap, see Gutterman, A. 2019. *Stakeholder Relationships and Engagement: A Guide for Sustainable Entrepreneurs*. Oakland CA: Sustainable Entrepreneurship Project; Gutterman, A. 2019. *Board Oversight of Sustainability: A Guide for Sustainable Entrepreneurs*. Oakland CA: Sustainable Entrepreneurship Project and Gutterman, A. 2020. *Sustainability Reporting and Communications*. New York, NY: Business Expert Press.

and philanthropy, and communications and public relations. TCB also distributes information through conferences, publications, case studies, webcasts, and podcasts.

Ethos Institute

The Ethos Institute of Business and Social Responsibility, based in Brazil (www.ethos.org.br), was created in 1998 by a group of private entrepreneurs and executives to mobilize, raise awareness, and help companies to run their business in a socially responsible manner, making them partners in building a just and sustainable society. The Ethos Institute has become a hub for knowledge organization, exchange of experiences, and development of tools to help companies analyze their management practices and deepen their commitment to social responsibility and sustainable development. The Ethos Institute aims to spread the practice of CSR, helping institutions to understand and progressively incorporate the concept of socially responsible business behavior; implement policies and practices that meet high ethical criteria, contributing to the achievement of long-term sustainable economic success; take responsibility for those affected by your activities; demonstrate to its shareholders the relevance of socially responsible behavior for the long-term return on their investments; identify innovative and effective ways of working in partnership with communities to build common welfare; and prosper, contributing to socially, economically, and environmentally sustainable development. The members of the Ethos Institute comprise companies of different segments and sizes, which account for annual revenues of approximately 35 percent of the Brazilian GDP and employ roughly two million people. The Ethos Institute has become a globally recognized leader in the promotion of CSR, forging partnerships with other organizations around the world, and its Ethos Indicators for Sustainable and Responsible Business have been widely recognized for their utility in assessing how sustainability and social responsibility have been incorporated into business and helping businesses to define sustainability strategies, policies, and processes.

Fundacion Entorno

The Entorno Foundation (http://fundacionentornos.org) is a civil society resource based in Spain that was created by academics who want to make available to the community, the experience acquired in public and research institutions, adding to the effort of national and international philanthropy to contribute to face the consequences that accelerated growth of urban environments is having on the health and welfare of citizens. The Foundation seeks to identify and propose, through research consistent with its mission, solutions to problems generated by the growth of cities, translating the results into best practices, policies, and planning resources for the construction of harmonic environments. The Foundation works with a number of other organizations under collaborative agreements and participates in training specialists in health, science, and technology.

Future-Fit Business Benchmark

The Future-Fit Foundation (futurefitbusiness.org) is a nonprofit organization whose vision is a future in which everyone on the Earth can flourish. Future-Fit is dedicated toward working for the achievement of a "Future-Fit society" that protects the possibility that humans and other life can flourish on Earth forever, by being environmentally restorative, socially just, and economically inclusive. Future-Fit has criticized actors in the global economy for failing to adequately address a host of critical environmental and social issues that are undermining the natural processes and social fabric that business, and society as a whole, relies upon.[17] Future-Fit argued that environmental and social challenges such as climate destabilization, ecosystems degradation, energy and water crises, food and health crises, infrastructure deterioration, financial inequality, education crises, and social instability must be addressed

---

[17] Future-Fit Business Framework, Part 1: Concepts, Principals and Goals (Future-Fit Foundation, Release 1, May 2016), 11, FutureFitBusiness.org.

by society, including businesses, in order for the planet to transition to a sustainable future.[18]

In furtherance of its goals and objectives, Future-Fit has developed the Future-Fit Business Benchmark as a free tool to help companies and investors transform how they create long-term value, for themselves and society as a whole, by operating within the boundaries of a set of eight system conditions.[19] In order to assist businesses in becoming "future-fit," the Benchmark proposed 21 Future-Fit business goals, which were derived by examining all of the ways that a "typical" company must seek to avoid breaching the Benchmark's business principles in the course of its actions with stakeholders.[20] The business goals were developed with reference to the issues, criteria, goals, and topics included in other well-regarded sustainability reporting and standards frameworks and companies should certain review and consider the goals included in standards such as the Global Reporting Initiative, B Lab's Impact Assessment, ISO 26000 Guidance on Social Responsibility, Corporate Knights Global

---

[18] For a list and fuller discussion of the "global challenges" identified by Future-Fit, see A. Gutterman, *Responsible Business: A Guide to Corporate Social Responsibility for Sustainable Entrepreneurs* (Oakland CA: Sustainable Entrepreneurship Project, 2019) available at www.seproject.org. See also Future-Fit Business Benchmark "Sources of Global Threats/Risks" and the additional sources of information listed thereon including "Expect the Unexpected: Building business value in a changing world," KPMG (2012); J. Rockstrom, W. Steffan et al., "Planetary Boundaries: Guiding human development on a changing planet," *Science* (January 2015), K. Raworth, "A Safe and Just Space for Humanity: Can we live within the doughnut,'" Oxfam Discussion Paper (February 2012); and "Global Opportunity Report 2015," Global Opportunity Network (2015).

[19] Future-Fit Business Framework, Part 1: Concepts, Principals and Goals (Future-Fit Foundation, Release 1, May 2016), 21, 25, FutureFitBusiness.org.

[20] The Future-Fit Business Benchmark described a "typical" company as follows: "Every company has an *Operational Presence* in or near local *Communities*. It sells goods or services to *Customers* who use and—for many types of physical goods— eventually dispose of them. Company operations rely on *Employees* and *Physical Resources*, which are often sourced from *Suppliers*. And how the company is run both depends upon and affects *Society as a Whole*." Id. at 28.

100, the Sustainability Accounting Standards Board, Integrated Reporting, and the United Nations Global Compact.[21]

Institute of Responsible Leadership

The Institute of Responsible Leadership (https://responsible-leadership.org/) is a not-for-profit organization based in London and launched in 2019 to seek to make the world a better place for private and public benefit. The Institute is dedicated to promoting leadership integrity resonant with CSR and sustainability in the public and private sector; offering courses/seminars, accreditation, mentoring, coaching, and consultancy in responsible leadership; providing high-quality IRL input and facilitation through founding members and associates; honoring and publicizing key examples of responsible leadership through the award of fellowships; and promoting a charter on responsible leadership for companies and other organizations. In conjunction with the Corporate Social Responsibility Finance Institute and the UN Institute for Teaching and Research, the institute holds regular seminars and workshops, as well as providing coaching/mentoring, accreditations, and research/advisory support.

International Business Leaders Forum Global

Founded in 1990, IBLF Global (www.iblfglobal.org) is an independent, not-for-profit global organization working with business leaders to deliver innovative solutions to sustainable development challenges worldwide. IBLF Global's mission is to engage in development activities around the world, thereby contributing to sustainable economic growth, raising business standards and influencing social development. Through collective action, partnerships, educational and thought leadership projects, IBLF Global works with a large network of multinational companies around

---

[21] See "Future-Fit Business Benchmark: Mapping of Future-Fit Benchmark Goals to Issues, Criteria, Goals and Topics Included in Other Sustainability Reporting and Standards Frameworks." Available FutureFitBusiness.org.

the world to encourage responsible business in the markets in which they are operating. IBLF Global supports international companies in their key markets to implement responsible business practices, build trust, and reduce corruption and reputation risk while working to create a level playing field. IBLF Global's business model is a small headquarters for project initiation and coordination, knowledge sharing, and local capacity building, with most actual project work carried out by local partners working with IBLF Global's experienced team of cross-sector facilitators. IBLF Global is an independent NGO, registered as a charity.

Oxfam

Oxfam (oxfam.org) is an international confederation of 19 organizations working together with partners and local communities in more than 90 countries to fight poverty and injustice. Oxfam seeks to find and implement practical, innovative ways for people to lift themselves out of poverty and thrive and seeks to engage in campaigns that ensure that the voices of the poor influence the local and global decisions that affect them. Oxfam works on interconnected issues like human rights, emergency response, and sustainable development.

Prince of Wales's Corporate Leaders Group

The Prince of Wales's Corporate Leaders Group (www.corporateleadersgroup.com/) is a select group of European business leaders working together under the patronage of The Prince of Wales to advocate solutions on climate change to policy makers and business peers within the EU and globally. Groups are convened by the University of Cambridge Institute for Sustainability Leadership and bring together business leaders from a range of sectors committed to supporting the transformation to competitive, sustainable, inclusive economies that will deliver net-zero carbon emissions by 2050. Through exchange of evidence-based ideas and influential discussions with policy makers and peers, the Corporate Leaders Groups advocate for robust business and policy solutions to the environmental and sustainability challenges facing our planet.

Social Accountability International

Social Accountability International (SAI) (www.sa-intl.org) was founded in 1997 and has grown to become a global nongovernmental organization advancing human rights at work and pursuing a vision of a world in which workers, business, and communities everywhere thrive together based on an understanding that socially responsible workplaces benefit business while securing fundamental human rights. SAI is a leader in policy and implementation, working together with a diverse group of stakeholders, including brands, suppliers, governments, trade unions, nonprofits, and academia. SAI has become widely known for the SA8000 Standard, which is the leading social certification standard for factories and organizations across the globe established as a multistakeholder initiative that helps certified organizations demonstrate their dedication to the fair treatment of workers across industries and in any country. SA8000, which is regularly revised, measures social performance in eight areas important to social accountability in workplaces (i.e., child labor, forced or compulsory labor, health and safety, freedom of association and right to collective bargaining, discrimination, disciplinary practices, working hours, and remuneration) and includes a management system element that drives continuous improvement in all areas of the Standard. In addition to publishing SA8000 and supporting documents, SAI offers a wide selection of resources including capacity building, stakeholder engagement, collaboration between buyers, and suppliers and the development of tools to ensure continued improvement. Companies are encouraged to pursue certification to the SA8000 Standard through accredited third-party certification bodies as a critical element contributing to their broader objectives of improving global labor conditions.

World Business Council for Sustainable Development

The World Business Council for Sustainable Development (WBCSD) (www.wbcsd.org) is a global, CEO-led organization of over 200 leading businesses working together to accelerate the transition to a sustainable world. WBCSD strives to help make member companies more successful and sustainable by focusing on the maximum positive impact for shareholders, the environment, and societies. Member companies come from all business sectors and all major economies, representing combined revenue of more than $8.5 trillion and 19 million employees as of 2019. WBCSD supports a Global Network of almost 70 national business councils that gives members unparalleled reach across the globe. WBCSD target the realization of the Sustainable Development Goals through six work programs to achieve systems transformation: redefining value, people, circular economy, food and nature, climate and energy, and cities and mobility. WBCSD conducts multiple projects in each of the program areas and also publishes papers, articles, tools, and case studies and convenes conferences that are attended by multiple stakeholders.

Environmental Organizations

Nonprofits and NGOs have made a significant impact on environmental and sustainable development issues including research, financial and technical assistance, consumer awareness, advocacy, and conservation-focused innovation.[22] Since environmental challenges transcend borders, NGOs have been particularly effective; however, many of the best run and successful organizations are locally based nonprofits that conduct most of their activities in their immediate communities.[23]

---

[22] Experts in the area of sustainable development asked in 2019 to name the NGOs that were making the greatest contribution to advancing progress on sustainable development identified the following NGOs most frequently: World Wildlife Fund, Greenpeace, World Resources Institute, Oxfam, The Nature Conservancy, Ceres, World Business Council for Sustainable Development, Ellen McArthur Foundation, and Environmental Defense Fund. The most common elements of NGO leadership mentioned by the experts included stakeholder engagement and collaboration, activism and advocacy, and innovation, knowledge, and taking a science-based approach. Why NGOs top the list of those advancing sustainable development (August 10, 2019), https://greenbiz.com/article/why-ngos-top-list-those-advancing-sustainable-development.

[23] Certain of the information on the sustainability-focused nonprofits and NGOs included in this chapter is adapted from various sources including the following: https://sustainabilitydegrees.com/blog/most-influential-sustainability-ngos/; https://healthline.com/health/best-nonprofits-sustainability#7; and https://cornucopia.org/2014/06/10-environmental-nonprofit-organizations-changing-world/

CDP

CDP (cdp.net) is a not-for-profit charity that runs the global disclosure system for investors, companies, cities, states, and regions to manage their environmental impacts and risk and opportunities on climate change, water security, and deforestation. To catalyze collective action toward its goals, CDP supports many different initiatives and has forged strong alliances around the world. CDP works with intergovernmental agencies, governments, business and regional associations, NGOs, and financial organizations around the world to drive further action. In addition, in order to support companies on their journey to environmental leadership, CDP has teamed up with external solutions providers to provide support in improving disclosures.

Conservation International

Conservation International (CI) (conservation.org) works to spotlight and secure the critical benefits that nature provides to humanity. CI works with scientists, local communities, and practitioners in the field to protect nature, global biodiversity, and human communities, and strives to protect natural wealth, promote sustainable business, and foster effective governance. CI has supported the creation, expansion, and improved management of nearly 50 million acres of marine and terrestrial protected areas in more than 70 countries. CI has offices in almost 30 countries and works with 2,000 partners around the globe.

Environmental Defense Fund

The Environmental Defense Fund (edf.org) is focused on addressing today's most urgent environmental challenges by working in partnership with others to target key issues such as moving to a 100 percent clean economy by putting a limit on climate pollution and spurring innovation; expanding sustainable fishing globally; increasing ecosystem resilience to meet demands for food, water and shelter in ways that allow people and nature to prosper in a changing climate; and reduce exposure to pollutants and toxic chemicals.

Green America

Green America (greenamerica.org) is focused on harnessing economic power—the strength of consumers, investors, businesses, and the market-place—to create a socially just and environmentally sustainable society. Green America's vision is a world where all people have enough, where all communities are healthy and safe and where the bounty of the Earth is preserved for all the generations to come. Green America works in four areas for system transformation including climate and clean energy, sustainable food and agriculture, responsible investing and fair labor and has created strategic programs relating to consumer education and mobilization (encouraging consumers to spend on green products and services, Green Business Network (encouraging businesses to adopt eco-friendly practices) and the Center for Sustainability Solutions.

Greenpeace

Greenpeace (greenpeace.org) is an environmental NGO with offices in over 39 countries and an international coordinating body in Amsterdam. Greenpeace describes itself as a global, independent campaigning organization that uses peaceful protest and creative communication to expose global environmental problems and promote solutions that are essential to a green and peaceful future. Since Greenpeace was created in 1971, it has been involved in a variety of causes and projects including bans on commercial whaling, convincing world leaders to stop nuclear testing and protection of Antarctica. Greenpeace does not solicit contributions from government or corporations, nor does it endorse political candidates. The organization's 250,000 members in the United States and 2.8 million members worldwide provide virtually all of its funding through individual contributions.

International Institute for Sustainable Development

The International Institute for Sustainable Development (iisd.org) (IISD) is an award-winning independent think tank championing solutions to the planet's greatest sustainability challenges and working with policy makers and private businesses toward a vision of a balanced world where people and the planet thrive. IISD's mission is to accelerate solutions that drive a global transition to fair economies, clean water, and a stable climate and its work is carried out in nearly 100 countries through core and project funding support from numerous governments inside and outside Canada, United Nations agencies, foundations, and the private sector. IISD's work is organized around six programs: economic law and policy, energy, reporting services, resilience, SDG knowledge, and water.

Natural Resources Defense Council

The National Resources Defense Council (NRDC) (nrdc.org) works to safeguard the Earth, its people, its plants, and animals, and the natural systems on which all life depends, and combines the power of more than three million members and online activists with the expertise of some 600 scientists, lawyers, and policy advocates across the globe to ensure the rights of all people to the air, the water, and the wild. The NRDC works with businesses, elected officials, and community groups in the United States and around the globe on important sustainability issues such as global warming, clean energy, reviving the world's oceans, defending endangered wildlife and wild places, pollution prevention, ensuring safe and sufficient water, and fostering sustainable communities.

Nature Conservancy

The Nature Conservancy (TNC) (nature.org) is a global environmental nonprofit working to create a world where people and nature can thrive. Founded at its grassroots in the United States in 1951, TNC has grown to become one of the most effective and wide-reaching environmental organizations in the world with more than a million members and impactful marine conservation projects involving more than 400 scientists in 72 countries across six continents.

Ocean Conservancy

Ocean Conservancy (oceanconservancy.org) works to protect the ocean from today's greatest global challenges by creating science-based solutions for a healthy ocean and the wildlife and communities that depend on it. One of its signature initiatives has been the International Coastal Cleanup program, which has removed hundreds of millions of pounds of trash from the world's beaches.

Oil and Gas Climate Initiative

The Oil and Gas Climate Initiative (OGCI) (oilandgasclimateinitiative. com) is a voluntary CEO-led initiative taking practical actions on climate change. OGCI members leverage their collective strength to lower carbon footprints of energy, industry, transportation value chains via engagements, policies, investments, and deployment. OGCI companies have established aggressive targets to reduce the collective average methane intensity of their aggregated upstream gas and oil operations and have pledged to work toward near zero methane emissions from the full gas value chain including transport and distribution to final customers. In addition, OGCI members companies support the aims of Zero Routine Flaring by 2030. OGCI members have also announced their intent to expand in the future independent third party verification, as applicable, on data published in OGCI's annual report.

Rainforest Alliance

The Rainforest Alliance (rainforest-alliance.org) is an international non-profit organization working at the intersection of business, agriculture, and forests to make responsible business the new normal, and has helped to forge an alliance of companies, farmers, foresters, communities, and consumers committed to creating a world where people and nature thrive in harmony. The organization works to conserve biodiversity and ensure sustainable livelihoods by transforming land-use practices, business practices, and consumer behavior. Among other things, the Alliance works with the agriculture, forestry, and tourism industries to change their practices and offers sustainability training around the world.

Rocky Mountain Institute

The Rocky Mountain Institute (RMI) (rmi.org) was founded in 1982 to pursue a mission of transforming global energy use to create a clean, prosperous, and secure low-carbon future. RMI has achieved global reach and reputation and engages businesses, governments, communities, academic and nonprofit institutions, and entrepreneurs to accelerate the adoption of market-based solutions that cost-effectively shift from fossil fuels sustainable, low-carbon energy sources.

Sierra Club

The Sierra Club (sierraclub.org) was founded in 1892 by conservationist John Muir and has thrived to become one of the oldest, largest, and most influential grassroots environmental organization in the United States with over 3.5 million members and supporters. The Sierra Club has protected millions of acres of wilderness and helped to draft and pass key environmental legislation in the United States including Clean Air Act, the Clean Water Act, and the Endangered Species Act. Other areas in which the Sierra Club has been active include moving away from the use of fossil fuels to clean energy, preservation and promotion of national parks and collecting money for community-led efforts to help hurricane recovery.

Science-Based Targets Initiative

The Science Based Targets Initiative (sciencebasedtargets.org) champions science-based target setting as a powerful way of boosting companies' competitive advantage in the transition to the low-carbon economy. The Initiative is a collaborative effort among CDP, the UN Global Compact, World Resources Institute, and the World Wide Fund for Nature and one of the We Mean Business Coalition commitments. The Initiative showcases companies that set science-based targets through case studies, events, and media to highlight the increased innovation, reduced regulatory uncertainty, strengthened investor confidence, and improved profitability and competitiveness generated by science-based target setting; defines and promotes best practice in science-based target setting with the support of a Technical Advisory Group; offers resources, workshops, and guidance to reduce barriers to adoption; and independently assesses and approves companies' targets.

350.org

350.org (350.org) is an international campaign dedicated to fighting climate change that was founded in 2008 with the goal of building a global climate movement. The organization was named after 350 parts per million, which was the safe concentration of carbon dioxide in the atmosphere at the time of founding (the level is now 400 parts per million and increasing by two parts per million each year). 350.org works on grassroots campaigns in almost 190 countries around the globe: from opposing coal plants and mega-pipelines, to supporting renewable energy solutions and cutting financial ties of the fossil fuel industry.

Union of Concerned Scientists

The Union of Concerned Scientists (ucsusa.org) is a national nonprofit organization founded 50 years ago by scientists and students at the Massachusetts Institute of Technology who sought to use the power of science to address global problems and improve people's lives. The organization puts rigorous, independent science to work to solve our planet's most pressing problems and has recruiting a group of nearly 250 scientists, analysts, and policy and communications experts to provide technical analysis and effective advocacy to create innovative, practical solutions for a healthy, safe, and sustainable future. Supported by contributions from hundreds of thousands of citizens, the Union of Concerned Scientists has helped establish higher fuel-efficiency requirements for vehicles and pass renewable-energy standards in many U.S. states.

UN Watch

UN Watch (unwatch.org) is an NGO established in 1993 and based in Geneva, Switzerland, whose mandate is to monitor the performance of the UN by the yardstick of its own Charter. UN Watch believes in the UN's mission on behalf of the international community to "save succeeding generations from the scourge of war" and provide for a more just world, and believes that even with its shortcomings, the UN remains an indispensable tool in bringing together diverse nations and cultures. Areas of interest for UN Watch include: UN management reform, the

UN and civil society, equality within the UN, and the equal treatment of member states. UN Watch, together with 20 other international NGOs, organizes each year the Geneva Summit for Human Rights and Democracy, which brings together well-known human rights defenders, victims, activists, and former political prisoners and is reported by major media around the world. UN Watch is a leader at the UN in the struggle against anti-Semitism, and campaigns at world bodies against all forms of racism and discrimination.

Wildlife Conservation Society

The Wildlife Conservation Society (WCS) (wcs.org) is dedicated to conservation of the world's largest wild places in 16 priority regions, home to more than 50 percent of the world's biodiversity. Among other things, WCS funds scientists who study ecosystems in the environment and works with governments, communities, businesses, and indigenous people to protect wildlife all over the world and pass and protect legislation that conserves animal habitats.

World Resources Institute

The World Resources Institute (WRI) (wri.org) is a global research organization that spans more than 60 countries including offices in the United States, China, India, Brazil, and Indonesia. The WRI has more than 1,000 experts and staff work closely with leaders to turn big ideas into action to sustain the world's natural resources—the foundation of economic opportunity and human well-being. The stated mission of the WRI is to move human society to live in ways that protect Earth's environment and its capacity to provide for the needs and aspirations of current and future generations. The work of the WRI focuses on seven critical issues and global challenges at the intersection of environment and development that need to be addressed in order to reduce poverty, grow economies, and protect natural systems:

- *Climate:* Protect communities and natural ecosystems from damage caused by greenhouse gas emissions, and generate opportunities for people by catalyzing a global transition to a low-carbon economy.

- *Energy:* Drive the scale-up of clean, affordable power systems throughout the world to deliver sustainable socio-economic development.
- *Food:* Ensure the world's food systems reduce their impact on the environment, drive economic opportunity, and sustainably feed 9.6 billion people by 2050.
- *Forests:* Alleviate poverty, enhance food security, conserve biodiversity, and mitigate climate change by reducing forest loss and restoring productivity to degraded, deforested lands.
- *Water:* Achieve a water-secure future by mapping, measuring, and mitigating global water risks.
- *Sustainable Cities:* Improve quality of life in cities by developing and scaling environmentally, socially, and economically sustainable urban and transport solutions.
- *The Ocean:* Charting the path for a New Ocean Economy that is good for jobs, economic growth, and human health while protecting and restoring the ocean.

World Wildlife Fund

Operating for almost 60 years, the World Wildlife Fund (WWF) (worldwildlife.org) is one of the most widely known sustainability nonprofits and has become the world's leading conservation organization with projects in about 100 countries that are supported by one million members in the United States and close five million members globally. The projects undertaken by WWF are focused on conservation of forests, fresh water, oceans, wildlife, food and climate for human and animals and WWF prides itself on its foundation in science to deliver innovative solutions that meet the needs of both people and nature.

Human Rights Organizations

Many believe that all of the subjects commonly associated with social responsibility are fundamentally issues of human rights. As such, it is no surprise that human rights are the primary focus of many of the most well-known nonprofits and NGOs. The compilation of organizations mentioned below is by no means all-inclusive and has been compiled based on various publicly available assessments of public recognition and reputation.[24] However, businesses interested in collaborating with nonprofits fighting for social justice may look to other organizations such as the American Civil Liberties Union Foundation, Black Youth Project, Fair Immigration Reform Network, Lawyers' Committee for Human Rights, National Organization for Women, Planned Parenthood, Task Force for Global Health, or Southern Poverty Law Center.

Amnesty International

Amnesty International (amnesty.org) is a global movement of more than 7 million people who take injustice personally and who want to be involved supporting research, advocacy, lobbying, campaigns, and action to create a world where human rights are enjoyed by all. While the organization has traditionally been based in London, it now operates primarily out of regional offices in cities in Africa, Asia-Pacific, Central and Eastern Europe, Latin America, and the Middle East, which serve as hubs for investigations, campaigns, and communications and support national sections in more than 70 countries. The organization's website includes detailed information on issues and topics of interest including armed conflict, climate change, corporate accountability, discrimination, indigenous peoples, sexual and reproductive rights, and the Universal Declaration of Human Rights. The organization is financed largely by fees and donations from citizens around the world, but has also received grants from governmental bodies.

Association for Women Rights in Development

Association for Women Rights in Development (AWID) (awid.org) is a global, feminist, membership, movement-support organization dedicated to support feminist, women's rights, and gender justice movements to

---

[24] See, e.g., https://topnonprofits.com/lists/best-nonprofits-on-the-web/; http://top10for.com/top-10-famous-human-rights-organizations-world/; and https://fundsforngos.org/featured-articles/worlds-top-ten-human-rights-organisations/

thrive, to be a driving force in challenging systems of oppression, and to cocreate feminist realities. AWID advances its work through influencing, advocacy, and campaigning; convening and connecting; solidarity and bridge-building; and arts and creative expression.

Business and Human Rights Centre

The Business and Human Rights Resource Centre (http://bhrrc.org/) is an international nonprofit organization which, as of 2019, was tracking the human rights impacts (positive and negative) of over 9,000 companies operating in over 180 countries worldwide. The Centre engages with companies and governments to urge them to share information publicly (and provides companies with opportunities to present their stories in full) and assists and supports communities and NGOs in getting companies to address human rights concerns. The Centre's regional researchers, located all over the world, go to local communities to understand the impacts of businesses on the ground, and regularly talk with business-people and government officials. The Centre releases briefings and analysis and serves as a global knowledge hub for resources and guidance for actions that businesses can take with respect to respecting and protecting human rights. The Centre's website delivers news in eight languages and includes guidance materials on a wide range of "big issues,"[25] cases and responses based on contacts with companies, examples of good practice and a database of company human rights policies. The Centre is committed to fair disclosure of all sides of debates on business and human rights issues and is independent of any government, religion, or political and economic interest, refusing to accept donations from companies, company foundations, or senior executives of corporations.

Child Rights International Network

The Child Rights International Network (CRIN) (crin.org) is an international not-for-profit organization based in London, which produces

---

[25] Among the "big issues" are mandatory due diligence, technology and human rights, social auditing, modern slavery, corporate legal accountability, climate justice, UN Guiding Principles, natural resources, and tax avoidance.

new research and thinking on human rights issues, with a focus on children's rights. The immediate role of CRIN is to fight for a world where children's rights are recognized, respected, and enforced, and where every rights violation has a remedy. The CRIN uses the UN Convention on the Rights of the Child as a starting point and works on many issues including the survival of the planet for new generations of children, institutional sexual violence, life imprisonment, and the death penalty, children's right to vote, and freedom of expression. CRIN works with international institutions like the UN, as well as governments, professionals and activists. CRIN undertakes legal research and supports children's rights activists by providing information, resources, and toolkits on a range of children's rights issues. In some circumstances and on particular issues, CRIN is able to provide direct support to children's rights activists, such as legal advocacy support or sharing its processes for how we work on certain issues.

Doctors Without Borders

Doctors Without Borders (doctorswithoutborders.org), which was awarded the Nobel Peace Prize in 1999, provides emergency medical aid to people affected by conflict, epidemics, disasters, or exclusion from health care and has treated tens of millions of people in over 80 countries since it was formed in 1971.

Ethical Trading Initiative

For over 20 years, the Ethical Trading Initiative (ETI) (https://ethical trade.org/) has worked to influence business to act responsibly and promote decent work. Taking a unique approach to business and human rights, members of the ETI are forward-thinking companies, trade unions, and NGOs working together to tackle the complex challenges of today's global supply chains to improve the lives of workers worldwide. ETI's activities include defining best practices in ethical trade by requiring all corporate members to agree to adopt the ETI Base Code of Labor Practice, which is based on the standards of the ILO, and developing a portfolio of the most effective steps companies can take to implement the

Base Code in their supply chains; helping workers to help themselves by supporting initiatives that raise workers' awareness of their rights, helping create work cultures where workers can confidently negotiate with management about the issues that concern them and brokering resolutions where there are major breaches of trade union rights by companies that supply ETI members; building strategic alliances in key sourcing countries and internationally to address problems that occur not only in individual workplaces, but also affect entire countries and industries; raising awareness of how governments, employers, trade unions, consumers, and the media can play a part in protecting workers' rights; working closely with governments and international labor agencies to influence policy and legislation; and driving improvements in member's ethical trade performance by requiring them to report annually on their efforts and the results they are achieving at farm or factory level.

Fair Labor Association

Formed in 1999, the Fair Labor Association (FLA) (www.fairlabor.org), a collaborative effort of socially responsible companies, colleges, and universities and civil society organizations (CSOs), has helped improve the lives of millions of workers around the world by creating lasting solutions to abusive labor practices by offering tools and resources to companies, delivering training to factory workers and management, conducting due diligence through independent assessments, and advocating for greater accountability and transparency from companies, manufacturers, factories, and others involved in global supply chains. The FLA believes that all goods should be produced fairly and ethically and has helped improve workers' lives by holding affiliated companies accountable for implementing FLA's Code of Conduct across their supply chains; conducting external assessments so that consumers can be assured of the integrity of the products they buy; and creating a space for CSOs to engage with companies and other stakeholders to find viable solutions to labor concerns.

One of the FLA's most notable achievements has been the development of its Code of Conduct, or Workplace Code, that includes standards that are based on ILO standards and internationally recognized good labor practices. Companies affiliated with the FLA are expected to comply with all relevant and applicable laws and regulations of the country in which workers are employed and to implement the Workplace Code in their applicable facilities. When differences or conflicts in standards arise, affiliated companies are expected to apply the highest standard. The FLA monitors compliance with the Workplace Code by carefully examining adherence to the FLA's Compliance Benchmarks, which identify specific requirements for meeting each Code standard, and the FLA's Principles of Monitoring, which guide the assessment of compliance.

Global Rights

Global Rights (globalrights.org) is an international human rights capacity-building NGO based in Africa, but also with activities in Asia and Latin America, which seeks to challenge injustice and amplify the voices of grassroots activists to promote, protect, and fulfill human rights. Global Rights exists to document and expose violations human rights, conduct community education and mobilization, advocate for legal and policy reform, use the courts as well as traditional means of dispute resolution on behalf of disadvantaged populations and engage the international community (including the United Nations and regional bodies) in critical human rights issues. Global Rights' programs address governance failures that exacerbate the disenfranchisement and the violations of the rights of the poor and marginalized, women and victims of discrimination and the organization focuses on access to justice, security and human rights, women's rights and gender equality and natural resources and human rights.

Human Rights Foundation

The Human Rights Foundation (HRF) (hrf.org) is a nonpartisan, nonprofit organization with a mission of uniting the world against tyranny and ensuring that freedom is both preserved and promoted around the world. HRF focuses its work on the founding ideals of the human rights movement most purely represented in the 1948 Universal Declaration of Human Rights and the 1976 International Covenant on Civil and

Political Rights. HRF partners with world-changing activists to defend, equip, and give them a platform to boldly change their communities and countries; creates innovative solutions by connecting activists to industry leaders and developing modern solutions to combat the worst human rights violations; and activates millions of supporters and amplifies the impact of their activities by inspiring people around the world to participate in the HRF's initiatives.

Human Rights Watch

Human Rights Watch (hrw.org) investigates and reports on abuses happening in all corners of the world using a team of roughly 450 people of 70-plus nationalities who are country experts, lawyers, journalists, and others who work to protect the most at risk, from vulnerable minorities and civilians in wartime, to refugees and children in need. The organization directs its advocacy toward governments, armed groups, and businesses, pushing them to change or enforce their laws, policies, and practices. To ensure its independence, Human Rights Watch refuses government funding and corporate ties, but does partner with organizations large and small across the globe to protect embattled activists and to help hold abusers to account and bring justice to victims.

International Committee of the Red Cross

Established in 1863, the International Committee of the Red Cross (ICRC) (icrc.org) operates worldwide, helping people affected by conflict and armed violence and promoting the laws that protect victims of war. An independent and neutral organization ensuring humanitarian protection and assistance for victims of war and armed violence, its mandate stems essentially from the Geneva Conventions of 1949. The ICRC is based in Geneva, Switzerland, employs some 16,000 people in more than 80 countries and is funded mainly by voluntary donations from governments and from National Red Cross and Red Crescent Societies. The International Red Cross and Red Crescent Movement is the largest humanitarian network in the world. Its mission is to alleviate human suffering, protect life and health, and uphold human dignity, especially during armed conflicts and other emergencies. It is present in every country and supported by millions of volunteers.

International Federation for Human Rights

The International Federation for Human Rights (FIDH) (fidh.org) is an international human rights NGO federating 184 organizations from 112 countries. Since 1922, FIDH has been defending all civil, political, economic, social, and cultural rights as set out in the Universal Declaration of Human Rights. FIDH acts at national, regional, and international levels in support of its member and partner organizations to address human rights abuses and consolidate democratic processes. Its work is directed at States and those in power, such as armed opposition groups and multinational corporations. Its primary beneficiaries are national human rights organizations who are members of FIDH, and through them, the victims of human rights violations. FIDH also cooperates with other local partner organizations and actors of change.

International Rescue Committee

The International Rescue Committee (rescue.org) responds to the world's worst humanitarian crises and helps people whose lives and livelihoods are shattered by conflict and disaster to survive, recover, and gain control of their future. In more than 40 countries and in 26 U.S. cities, the Committee's dedicated teams provide clean water, shelter, health care, education, and empowerment support to refugees and displaced people. Working with international partners, the Committee provides children with schooling and education opportunities; supports existing and new businesses; sponsors and participates in awareness-raising sessions on governance-related topics, such as individual rights, conflict mitigation, and local government hotlines; provides training on child protection, gender-based violence, and protection principles, and service delivery; raises awareness about human rights, protection and gender-based violence; supports village saving and loan association members; and supports schools, education centers, vocational training centers, and safe healing and learning spaces.

Office of the UN High Commissioner for Human Rights

The Office of the UN High Commissioner for Human Right (OHCHR) (ohchr.org) is the leading UN entity on human rights, entrusted by the General Assembly with a unique mandate to promote and protect all human rights for all people. The UN human rights program aims to ensure that the protection and enjoyment of human rights is a reality in the lives of all people. OHCHR also plays a crucial role in safeguarding the integrity of the three interconnected pillars of the UN: peace and security, human rights, and development. OHCHR is part of the United Nations Secretariat, with a staff of some 1,300 people and its headquarters in Geneva, as well as an office in New York, and provides assistance in the form of technical expertise and capacity-development in order to support the implementation of international human rights standards on the ground. It assists governments, which bear the primary responsibility for the protection of human rights, to fulfill their obligations and supports individuals to claim their rights. Moreover, it speaks out objectively on human rights violations. The Geneva-based headquarters has three substantive divisions:

- Thematic Engagement, Special Procedures, and Right to Development Division, which develops policy and provides guidance, tools, advice, and capacity-strengthening support on thematic human rights issues, including for human rights mainstreaming purposes; and provides support to the Human Rights Council's special procedures.
- Human Rights Council and Treaty Mechanisms Division, which provides substantive and technical support to the HRC and the Council's UPR mechanism, and supports the human rights treaty bodies.
- Field Operations and Technical Cooperation Division, which is responsible for overseeing and implementing the OHCHR's work in the field.

The High Commissioner for Human Rights is the principal human rights official of the UN and heads OHCHR and spearheads the UN's human rights efforts.

Office of the UN High Commissioner for Refugees

The Office of the United Nations High Commissioner for Refugees was established on December 14, 1950, by the United Nations General Assembly. The Office is responsible for the operations of the UN Refugee Agency (unhcr.org), which is a global organization dedicated to saving lives, protecting rights, and building a better future for refugees, forcibly displaced communities, and stateless people and leading and coordinating international action to protect refugees and resolve refugee problems worldwide. The Agency has personnel in over 130 countries around the world and works to ensure that everybody has the right to seek asylum and find safe refuge, having fled violence, persecution, war, or disaster at home. Since 1950, the Agency has faced multiple crises on multiple continents, and provided vital assistance to refugees, asylum-seekers, internally displaced and stateless people, many of whom have nobody left to turn to. The Agency's goal is to help to save lives and build better futures for millions forced from home in a variety of ways including advocacy, providing critical emergency assistance in the form of clean water and health care, shelter, transport, assistance packages for people who return home and income-generating projects for those who resettle. In more than six decades, the Agency has helped tens of millions of people restart their lives.

Protection International

Protection International (PI) (protectioninternational.org) is an international nonprofit organization that supports human rights defenders in developing their security and protection management strategies. PI works with local partners in over 30 countries across the globe in Africa, Asia and Latin America to protect human rights defenders (HRDs) by piloting new methodologies and innovative approaches, through activities such as publishing the first manual on the protection of HRDs; providing systematic overviews on existing public policies initiatives for HRDs protection; developing security and protection tools for grassroot HRDs at risk; exploring innovative approaches for the self-protection of organizations and communities based on this experience; and contributing to the recognition of HRDs as actors of positive social change over the years.

Refugees International

Refugees International (RI) (refugeesinternational.org) advocates for lifesaving assistance and protection for displaced people and promotes solutions to displace crises. RI is an independent organization that does not accept any government or UN funding. RI was started in 1979 as a citizens' movement to protect Indochinese refugees. Since then, RI has expanded to become a leading advocacy organization that provokes action from global leaders to resolve refugee crises. RI's expert recommendations are highly valued by the very people whose decisions bring immediate relief and lifesaving solutions to refugees: senior officials of the U.S. administration and Congress, the UN, and governments around the world.

United for Human Rights

United for Human Rights (UHR) (humanrights.com) is an international nonprofit organization active in over 195 countries and dedicated to implementing the UN Declaration of Human Rights at local, regional, national, and international levels. Its membership is comprised of individuals, educators, and groups throughout the world who are actively forwarding the knowledge and protection of human rights by and for all mankind. Its purpose is to provide human rights educational resources and activities that inform, assist, and unite individuals, educators, organizations, and governmental bodies in the dissemination and adoption of the UN Declaration at every level of society.

UN Women

UN Women (unwomen.org) is the UN entity dedicated to gender equality and the empowerment of women. UN Women supports UN Member

States as they set global standards for achieving gender equality, and works with governments and civil society to design laws, policies, programs, and services needed to ensure that the standards are effectively implemented and truly benefit women and girls worldwide. UN Women works globally to make the vision of the Sustainable Development Goals a reality for women and girls and stands behind women's equal participation in all aspects of life, focusing on four strategic priorities: women lead, participate in, and benefit equally from governance systems; women have income security, decent work, and economic autonomy; all women and girls live a life free from all forms of violence; and women and girls contribute to and have greater influence in building sustainable peace and resilience, and benefit equally from the prevention of natural disasters and conflicts and humanitarian action. Working for the empowerment and rights of women and girls globally, UN Women's main roles are to support intergovernmental bodies, such as the Commission on the Status of Women, in their formulation of policies, global standards, and norms; to help Member States implement these standards, standing ready to provide suitable technical and financial support to those countries that request it, and to forge effective partnerships with civil society; and to lead and coordinate the UN system's work on gender equality, as well as promote accountability, including through regular monitoring of systemwide progress.

UNFPA United Nations Population Fund

UNFPA (unfpa.org), formerly the United Nations Population Fund, is the sexual and reproductive health agency of the UN pursuing a mission of delivering a world where every pregnancy is wanted, every child birth is safe and every young person's potential is fulfilled. Among other things, UNFPA supports reproductive health care for women and youth in more than 150 countries, which are home to more than 80 percent of the world's population; the health of pregnant women, especially the 1 million who face life-threatening complications each month; reliable access to modern contraceptives sufficient to benefit 20 million women a year; training of thousands of health workers to help ensure at least 90 percent of all childbirths are supervised by skilled attendants;

prevention of gender-based violence, which affects one in three women; and efforts to end child marriage, which could affect an estimated 70 million girls over the next five years. The organization was created in 1969, the same year the UN General Assembly declared "parents have the exclusive right to determine freely and responsibly the number and spacing of their children."

United Nations Development Programme

The United Nations Development Programme (undp.org) is active in about 170 countries and territories and working on eradicating poverty while protecting the planet by helping countries develop strong policies, skills, partnerships and institutions so they can sustain their progress. UNDP is working to strengthen new frameworks for development, disaster risk reduction and climate change and is supporting efforts to achieve the Sustainable Development Goals included in the 2030 Agenda for Sustainable Development through a set of Signature Solutions: keeping people out of poverty; governance for peaceful, just, and inclusive societies; crisis prevention and increased resilience; environment: nature-based solutions for development; clean, affordable energy; and women's empowerment and gender equality. The UNDP Administrator is the Vice-Chair of the UN Sustainable Development Group, which unites the funds, programs, specialized agencies, departments, and offices of the UN system that play a role in sustainable development. UNDP also administers the UN Capital Development Fund, which helps developing countries grow their economies by supplementing existing sources of capital assistance by means of grants and loans; and UN Volunteers, which fields over 6,500 volunteers from 160 countries, serving with 38 UN partners in support of peace, security, human rights, humanitarian delivery, and development through volunteerism worldwide.

United Nations Foundation

The United Nations Foundation (unfoundation.org) was founded in 1998 by entrepreneur and philanthropist Ted Turner to support the UN and serve as a strategic partner and resource for the UN in solving global problems. Turner's goals in establishing the foundation were to demonstrate the value of investing in the UN, encourage new partners to work with the UN, and promote strong U.S. leadership at the UN. In the first 20 years, the foundation mobilized over $2 billion, numerous initiatives, and countless partners to support the UN and UN causes. This support helped the UN pioneer work in areas we all now take for granted, from supporting elections to the rights of adolescent girls to our shared interest in a clean energy future for all. Today, the foundation focuses on mobilizing ideas, people, and resources to help the UN tackle some of the greatest collective action challenges of our time, including scaled collaboration to achieve the Sustainable Development Goals and the promise of the Paris Agreement on climate change.

United Nations International Children's Emergency Fund (UNICEF)

The United Nations Children's Fund (UNICEF) (unicef.org) works in over 190 countries and territories to save children's lives, to defend their rights and to help them fulfill their potential, from early childhood through adolescence. UNICEF's work spans a number of areas such as child protection and inclusion including initiatives relating to adolescent development, child protection, children uprooted, children with disabilities, environment and climate change, gender equality, and social inclusion; child survival including initiatives relating early childhood development, health, HIV/AIDS, immunization and nutrition; education including initiatives relating to children with disabilities, early childhood development, and innovation in education; gender equality; emergencies and humanitarian action for children; supply and logistics; research and analysis and learning and knowledge exchange.

World Health Organization (WHO)

The World Health Organization (WHO) (who.int) works worldwide to promote health, keep the world safe and serve the vulnerable with the goal of ensuring that a billion more people have universal health coverage, to protect a billion more people from health emergencies, and provide a further billion people with better health and well-being. For universal health coverage WHO focuses on primary health care to improve access to quality essential services, works toward sustainable financing and financial protection, improves access to essential medicines and health products, trains the health workforce and advise on labor policies, supports people's participation in national health policies and improves monitoring, data, and information. For health emergencies, WHO prepares for emergencies by identifying, mitigating, and managing risks, prevents emergencies, and supports development of tools necessary during outbreaks, detects and responds to acute health emergencies and supports delivery of essential health services in fragile settings. For health and well-being, WHO addresses social determinants, promotes intersectoral approaches for health, and prioritizes health in all policies and healthy settings. Through its work, WHO addresses human capital across the lifecourse, prevention of noncommunicable diseases, promotion of mental health, climate change in small island developing states, antimicrobial resistance, and elimination and eradication of high-impact communicable diseases. Formed in 1948, WHO now has more than 7,000 people from more than 150 countries working in 150 country offices, in six regional offices and at its headquarters in Geneva.

World Organization Against Torture

World Organization against Torture (OMCT) (omct.org) was created in 1985 and has emerged as the main coalition of international NGOs fighting against torture, summary executions, enforced disappearances and all other cruel, inhuman, or degrading treatment. With over 200 affiliated organizations in its SOS-Torture Network and many tens of thousands correspondents in every country, OMCT is the most important network of NGOs working for the protection and the promotion of human rights in the world. Based in Geneva, OMCT's International Secretariat provides personalized medical, legal, and/or social assistance to hundreds of torture victims and ensures the daily dissemination of urgent interventions across the world, in order to protect individuals and to fight against impunity. Specific OMCT programs allow it to provide support to specific categories of vulnerable people, such as women, children, and human rights defenders. OMCT also submits individual communications and alternative reports to the special mechanisms of the UN, and actively collaborates in the respect, development, and strengthening of international norms for the protection of human rights. OMCT enjoys a consultative status with ECOSOC (United Nations), the International Labour Organization, the African Commission on Human and Peoples' Rights, the Organisation Internationale de la Francophonie, and the Council of Europe.

About the Author

Alan S. Gutterman's prolific output of practical guidance and tools for legal and financial professionals, managers, entrepreneurs and investors has made him one of the best-selling individual authors in the global legal publishing marketplace. Alan has authored or edited over 90 books on sustainable entrepreneurship, leadership and management, business law and transactions, international law and business and technology management for a number of publishers. Alan has extensive experience as a partner and senior counsel with internationally recognized law firms counseling small and large business enterprises in the areas of general corporate and securities matters, venture capital, mergers and acquisitions, international law and transactions, strategic business alliances, technology transfers and intellectual property, and has also held senior management positions with several technology-based businesses. He received his AB, MBA., and JD from the University of California at Berkeley, a DBA from Golden Gate University, and a PhD from the University of Cambridge. For more information about Alan and his activities, please visit his website at alangutterman.com.

Index

OTHER TITLES IN THE ENVIRONMENTAL AND SOCIAL SUSTAINABILITY FOR BUSINESS ADVANTAGE COLLECTION

Robert Sroufe, Duquesne University, Editor

- *Strategic Planning for Sustainability* by Alan S. Gutterman
- *Sustainability Reporting and Communications* by Alan S. Gutterman
- *Sustainability Leader in a Green Business Era* by Amr E. Sukkar
- *Managing Sustainability* by John Friedman
- *Human Resource Management for Organizational Sustainability* by Radha R. Sharma
- *Climate Change Management* by Huong Ha
- *Social Development Through Benevolent Business* by Kalyan Sankar Mandal
- *ISO 50001 Energy Management Systems* by Johannes Kals
- *Feasibility Analysis for Sustainable Technologies* by Scott R. Herriott
- *The Role of Legal Compliance in Sustainable Supply Chains, Operations, and Marketing* by John Wood
- *The Thinking Executive's Guide to Sustainability* by Kerul Kassel
- *A Primer on Sustainability* by Ronald Whitfield and Jeanne McNett
- *IT Sustainability for Business Advantage* by Brian Moore
- *Developing Sustainable Supply Chains to Drive Value* by Robert Sroufe and Steven Melnyk
- *Developing Sustainable Supply Chains to Drive Value, Volume I* by Robert P. Sroufe and Steven A. Melnyk

Concise and Applied Business Books

The Collection listed above is one of 30 business subject collections that Business Expert Press has grown to make BEP a premiere publisher of print and digital books. Our concise and applied books are for...

- Professionals and Practitioners
- Faculty who adopt our books for courses
- Librarians who know that BEP's Digital Libraries are a unique way to offer students ebooks to download, not restricted with any digital rights management
- Executive Training Course Leaders
- Business Seminar Organizers

Business Expert Press books are for anyone who needs to dig deeper on business ideas, goals, and solutions to everyday problems. Whether one print book, one ebook, or buying a digital library of 110 ebooks, we remain the affordable and smart way to be business smart. For more information, please visit www.businessexpertpress.com, or contact sales@businessexpertpress.com.